PIG TALES

Stories of Law Enforcement

Robert Phillips

iUniverse

PIG TALES
STORIES OF LAW ENFORCEMENT

iUniverse books may be ordered through booksellers or by contacting:

iUniverse
1663 Liberty Drive
Bloomington, IN 47403
www.iuniverse.com
1-800-Authors (1-800-288-4677)

ISBN: 978-1-5320-5770-0 (sc)
ISBN: 978-1-5320-5771-7 (e)

Library of Congress Control Number: 2018911506

Print information available on the last page.

iUniverse rev. date: 09/24/2018

1

The Village Idiot

One might wonder why anyone with good sense would even attempt to obtain a job in law enforcement, much less want to write about it. Everyone else seems to have the same question. Why else would they send you to a psychiatrist when you are going through the hiring process for a job in law enforcement? They must believe you're nuts to want to do this stuff. After all, who else would line up to have people try to shoot them, knife them, run over them with vehicles, blow them up, sic dogs on them, verbally abuse them, threaten them with bodily harm, or have them fired? When I had the flash of genius to take the police exam, I heard five thousand people were taking the test. I had a score of 93.5, and when I received the results in the mail, I was informed I had placed 138th overall. I thought, *Hey, pretty good.*

I took the test because I had been laid off and needed a job. My wife was a civilian employee with the sheriff's office at the time. I would take her to lunch, sometimes take her to work, and pick her up after work. While doing this, I got to know the personnel in the office, and after a while, I began to think I could do this job. After I had been with the sheriff's office for just over eleven years, my dad (known in the family as Pop) told me he'd known even when I was a kid that I would get into law enforcement. I was afraid to ask him how he knew. He told me I had my mother's investigative skills. I never claimed to have good sense, and he has referred to me more than once as the village idiot.

I hope someone besides me reads this book. It's the best description I can give of being a law enforcement officer. I know in our politically correct world a few of these stories may offend some. If that's the case, too bad. I have nothing against anybody. I'm not leaving out the rich, the poor, the middle class, whites, blacks, Hispanics, Asians, males, females, or unknowns. I'm short, bald, and fat; I've got four eyes; I'm completely deaf in my left ear; and I can't hear well out of my right. I'm not the sharpest knife in the drawer, but I've never considered treating others unfairly just because they aren't like me. My parents taught me at a young age that there is good and bad in all people. I've always tried to treat people the way I want to be treated, but I would also treat them as they treated me.

Am I ranting yet?

After having the initial brainstorm to write this book, several questions occurred to me. What would I write about? Why would anyone want to read what I had written? After all, nobody would believe it, though nobody could make up this stuff. But since this is about me, I will tell you a little about myself. My life started when my parents, Charles and Ruth Phillips, celebrated Christmas 1961. I know this because I was born September 25, 1962, and you can do the math. I joke that if I had been a girl I would have been named Noel. I was the youngest child until January 1969, when Mom and Pop cranked up the baby factory again. In all, Mom and Pop had seven children, and my parents were married (to each other). For this reason I couldn't go to work for the FBI. That's a joke.

I guess my childhood was normal, but what standard can you use to determine that? My folks didn't drink (except for medicinal purposes), fight (at least not in front of us kids), or beat or abuse us. (Work or chores didn't count as abuse then.) We got to see our kinfolk regularly, and we always had food to eat. We moved a lot when I was a kid because Pop often changed jobs. I went to several schools, but I don't think I suffered too much damage because of that. I was a bit shy, possibly because of the moves and the new schools, and I am still a bit of a loner, but I had a few girlfriends during my school years, so how shy could I have been? I broke my hip when I was fifteen and because of this was not allowed to participate in sports during my high school years. I took music class and sang in the concert choir. I was voted class cutup and appeared in the senior play.

I've always felt I could be an entertainer if given the opportunity, but I probably wouldn't be as happy as I am now because of all the money and adulation forced on me. Instead I have chosen to risk my life for nearly thirty years for the praise that comes with this job. I hope you'll find this book as fun to read as I have found the job on most days. As you read it, I hope you'll wonder how one person could be so charmed.

I told you there had to be something wrong with anyone who wanted to do this job. I'm probably not the greatest deputy. I've never claimed to be, but I'm good at what I do. I'll probably never solve that big case or change the world, but I have been able to change my little piece of it for the better.

2

Time in the Pokey

When I started with the sheriff's office in April 1998, the reigning sheriff had been in office just a few months less than I had been in existence. I was born in September 1962, and he was first elected in November of that year. Holy cow! I was twenty-five years old. Incredibly enough, he would be elected two more times.

I'll never forget when I was hired. My wife was a civilian employee at the sheriff's office, and I had often spoken with a sergeant in the internal affairs division when I would take her to lunch. Like everyone else, he knew me as Robbie, the name Mom gave me. I've been called this all my life. I've tried to break people of the habit numerous times, but somebody always says, "Hey, Robbie," and then everybody uses that name. Most people grow out of shortened or altered versions of their names, but this one had always stuck. When my name,

Robert Edward Phillips, came up on the sheriff's office list, the sergeant called my wife to ask what her husband's name was. She said it was Robert Edward, and he told her to have me call him "because they decided to hire a white one." I don't think he meant anything bad by this, but I said some people could be offended.

At the time, the sheriff's office was hiring only for the jail, and I was fine with this because I had been laid off and was drawing pennies from unemployment, which was going to run out in about three weeks. I started on the day shift at the jail, which some would say was not bad for a new guy with no time or seniority. On my first day I learned what qualified me for the day shift. When I reported for duty, the senior day-shift sergeant asked me if I was in the National Guard or the reserves. When I told him no, he replied I would be a good man for the day shift. I don't recall him ever saying anything else to me.

I worked for about three weeks on the day shift before the sheriff's office sent me to the police academy. Training lasted seven weeks at the time. I think our guys now go through a sixteen-week academy, and I don't believe they're as well trained as we were. At least some of the new officers I've had dealings with aren't. The academy was okay. The book stuff was easy, but I was a little slow on the obstacle course. I said I was a fat boy. I always have been and probably always will be. I also made the mistake of listening to another deputy and taking a borrowed revolver to shoot. I was a good shot, but I'd always shot a semiautomatic. I couldn't shoot a revolver worth a flip, but I was told the guy who handled the firearms qualification hated semiautomatics and would probably try to fail me because I carried one. So I borrowed a revolver I'd never shot. Not a smart move. I barely qualified, in the middle to high seventies.

The academy director had no sense of humor. The academy had officers fill out an exit survey, and if they gave honest answers to certain questions, they would be called on the carpet and he would threaten to report them to their sheriff. Hey, if you can't take a joke, excuse me. After finishing the academy, which had nothing to teach about corrections, I worked in the jail for around two months and faced the first of many attempts on my life.

I had been with the sheriff's office for only a few weeks. The deputy who normally worked the floor had called in sick, and the deputy I was working with was called away. Inmate visitation was in progress, along with other daily business. (The store, a cart with food and other items, was available to inmates, and the Pepsi man and the coffee man were on the floor.) As with most jails, we have workers (inmates who do tasks such as cooking and cleaning) called trustees. On this day one of the trustees continued to call into the cube (the control room), wanting out of the block to talk with me about a problem. I had put him off a couple of times, but then he said he had a headache and asked for Tylenol, knowing we couldn't deny him medical attention. A large bottle of Tylenol was kept in the control room, where deputies worked.

The painkiller was to be dispensed whenever an inmate had a headache. Nowadays deputies aren't allowed to do anything like this. I had a stupid moment and told the inmate to come out and get two tablets. He approached the slider door, and I opened it to let him out. A lockable hatch is built into these doors, and after this incident, I used it on a regular basis. That day this one was closed and locked. The hatches unlock from the outside. I later learned other deputies like to keep the hatches locked because they're knee knockers. You may bump into them as you enter the control room, tearing your uniform trousers and cutting your knee.

As I opened the door, I was called on the two-way intercom; a visitor wanted to come to the floor to see an inmate. I turned to acknowledge the caller, and the trustee threw something around my neck in lasso fashion and put a shank (a homemade knife) to my throat. He told me to open another block and a cell where he was going to lock me up so he could escape. I opened the block and took one step into the hall. Another inmate, who had been a trustee but had been busted (fired) from working, entered the hallway. I thought he was in on the escape plan, but he waved his arms to distract my captor. I used this distraction to break away from the inmate, slammed the control room door, and locked it. (After all, the guy still had a knife.) After a couple of laps back and forth, the inmate ran toward his cell. I had closed all the other doors electronically. The potential escapee ran down the hall, picked up a chair, and raised it as if to hit the slider door (the main door leading to the floor), which was made out of metal and safety glass.

I yelled at him to put down the chair and to sit in one of the rooms in the hallway we used for attorney visits. He finally complied. After he had settled down and I had swallowed the big ball of air caught in my throat, I called downstairs and asked for someone to come up because of a problem with an inmate. The inmate was given time in the disciplinary block and charged with assault and attempted escape. Because of my stupidity (opening the door to the cube and not having the safety port open), I received five days off without pay. I spent most of that time playing a Nintendo game system my wife bought had me, and I had a very sore thumb by the end of the week. I figured I was probably charmed because that lump of air I'd swallowed could have leaked out from a big hole in my neck.

The only reason I could guess the second inmate helped me was that I would take the inmates to the rooftop exercise area, which had a full basketball court. The deputies didn't like to take the inmates there, but I was new and didn't mind. I got some fresh air while I was up there and away from the foul-smelling body odor that permeated the jail. This inmate had been there when he was in the trustee block.

It was later learned the other inmate had planned an escape for several weeks, waiting for a chance when just one deputy was working the floor. I guess it was my lucky day. He had made the knife from a toothbrush and razors he had bought at the jail store. He had heated the brush handle and had inserted the blades. He had managed to obtain tape from somewhere to secure them. He was sentenced to fifteen years for the incident, and I think he did about two or three. I saw him when he was coming through the jail again for his appeal. He wanted to apologize. He wasn't originally jailed for anything serious. He was involved in a check-writing scam in which the ink disappeared on the checks sometime after they were written.

After my suspension, I returned to work and received a transfer letter to our county's other jail. Our county has two county seats, so all services are duplicated. The transfer wasn't part of the disciplinary action against me. I know because my superiors told me it wasn't. That's a sheriff's office joke. They never give you a transfer in person. They wait until you are on vacation or on suspension.

3

Pranks at the Pebble

I went to work in the little jail, or the Pebble as I like to call it. If the main jail is the Rock, the little jail would naturally be the Pebble. I worked mostly on the night shift. When our county was created, it was so vast that years before residents of one part decided they wanted to secede and to start their own county. It was a day's ride by wagon from their area to the county seat. However, the state said they didn't have the landmass they needed, and none of the counties that touched this part of the county would give up any of their land. They would get nothing in return, so there was no benefit for them. The disgruntled residents decided if they couldn't get their own county they would have the next best thing. Our county is basically divided in two. We have two county seats, which means two courthouses, two jails, and two road and transportation departments. Fortunately we have only one set of county commissioners and one sheriff.

The night shift is a bit more relaxed. The brass isn't looking over your shoulder, and you have more time to be creative. Harmless fun helps you keep awake and pass the time. On the night shift our main job was to check blocks. One deputy was making checks, flying through the blocks with his flashlight. Unknown to him, I had let another deputy in one of the blocks to scare the heebie-jeebies out of him. This deputy hid in the shower in the inmate common area. When we came to work, the inmates would be in their cells unless a major sporting event was on TV. For these they were usually allowed to stay up later, but for the most part after about an hour the inmates were asleep. So one deputy was doing checks and another was hiding in a darkened block, ready for him. He hit that block, and when he passed her, she jumped out and shrieked like Janet Leigh in the shower scene from *Psycho*. When I get excited my voice goes up, but this guy gave new meaning to the term "screams like a girl." He went rigid and scooted across the floor backward. He later said he didn't scream, but inmates rang on the intercom to ask what those yeti noises were.

On another night this same deputy was sent to check on a possible window problem in one of the disciplinary cells. The same female deputy had gone up to the roof to hide outside the window. When he shined his light on the window, she jumped out, banging on the window and yelling. Once again he didn't scream. We're lucky he didn't crack the safety glass. This stuff is as funny to watch on the jail's camera system as it is in person. He wasn't the only person to get his heart checked at work.

Just after I went to work at the newly opened little jail, I started on the night shift. Although the old jail was closed, we still had access to it. I think it has been remodeled to provide courthouse offices. There was a bit of history to the old jail. During the civil rights marches in Birmingham in the sixties, Martin Luther King Jr. was arrested and held there. One of the old head sergeants thought it was something to take the new deputies on a tour of the jail to show them where King was held. One night I was talking with a new deputy who had been given the tour about how the old jail differed from the new one. I told him I had never seen the old jail, and he suggested we go over there. Another old head sergeant agreed too easily to let us go. He was known to be a practical joker. He told us how scary it was in the old jail at night. We grabbed a flashlight and off we went.

The deputy showed me where King had stood and recalled how the old head sergeant had made such a big deal out of this. We noted the differences between the old and the new jails. The deputy was demonstrating how the doors were opened in one of the blocks when suddenly out of the darkness a hand reached for us. A single flashlight wasn't providing enough light to protect us. I'll admit I was scared. I knew I had a strong heart, but just weeks earlier I'd had my heart checked with a razor to the throat. The deputy who was showing me around defined scared. He jumped a foot and a half, and like a cartoon character, he was running but not going anywhere. After he landed back on the ground and the terror was over, I thought he was going to club the sergeant with the flashlight. We laughed over this later, but I never returned to the old jail—too scary.

4

We Need Guns!

One night I was working the booking desk with a recently promoted sergeant. An alarm call came in at the courthouse credit union, and the jail was the contact for the alarm company. The two buildings were connected by a tunnel for court reasons. Workers inside the jail are unarmed, but we wore our uniforms and gun belts. When we got to work we locked our guns in a storage box.

When the alarm company called, as it often did, we usually contacted the patrol division, which would send a unit to check for any problem. The new sergeant, who had been working on the patrol division when he was promoted, said, "It's probably a false alarm. Come on. We'll go check it out." I grabbed a flashlight and waved at the deputy working the control room to open the outer door so I could get my gun, but the sergeant said, "You don't need that. We're just gonna walk over there, check it out, and be right back."

We went over to the courthouse and down a long dark hall. The audible alarm was going off, and we saw broken glass from the credit union door on the floor. Someone had also broken into one of the court offices. I'll never forget the look on the sergeant's face as he stopped in the hallway, the smoke from his cigarette circling his head, and said in monotone, "We need guns." He had to go back to contact the patrol division because walkie-talkie radios had not been issued to jail personnel at that time. He posted me with flashlight in hand as "security" until he returned. I told him later it would have taken me one second to get that gun I wanted to carry. He agreed. Hindsight, huh? To this day when I see him, I mimic smoking a cigarette, look at him, and say, "We need guns."

5

Love Letters from Abroad and from the County Jail

There were a lot of slow nights in the little jail, but I didn't complain. The one time I commented about how slow the night had been, we paid dearly for it the very next night by getting eight inmates in for booking and processing. We usually got four a week. On slow nights we found ways to entertain ourselves, sometimes by writing letters. At the time our jail had a free-mail day. Inmates could send letters, and the county paid the postage. This was usually on Sunday. One self-promoting suck-up of a deputy would read the inmate mail word for word. The brown-nosing paid off for him because he shot through the ranks.

Most of the letters were fairly boring. We thought we would jazz up a letter for him one night. Another deputy, who had terrible penmanship, did the writing, and I told him what to write. We made up an elaborate escape plan and dropped the letter in the cellblock so when this guy did a block check he would find the letter but wouldn't be able to tell which cell it had come from. On a block check, a deputy walks through the cellblocks with a flashlight and makes sure no one has decided to escape by tunneling out or by hanging himself.

Just like clockwork, this deputy came bouncing through checking cells and gathering mail. Then he went back downstairs as he always did and started reading. He found the escape plan and called upstairs to find out if we knew which cell door it had been slid under. To make the letter look real, we included a code and signed it with a nickname. We also misspelled some words. This guy spent most of the night trying to find out which inmate(s) were planning an escape. He even pulled store signature cards and booking cards to compare handwriting. We finally told him what was up because we worked eight-hour shifts and wanted to go home when the shift was over.

That wasn't the only writing we did while doing time. We wrote a lot of letters transferring people to different shifts when they wanted to go or when they didn't. We did the same with patrol division transfers. It was always funny to watch someone come in after an off day and find a letter pinned to the bulletin board. Everyone knew the people in administration never made a personnel move while we were at work. They waited until we had a day off or were on vacation. Then they made a transfer or put up a disciplinary letter.

One night we wanted to write somebody a letter. We decided a love letter would be perfect. After all, we had a couple of women working with us and they probably needed fan mail. We wrote a steamy love letter to a female deputy, put an inmate's name on it, and made sure she got the note. The ink wasn't dry when she came up to the floor demanding that the inmate be brought out. I believe she was going to kick his butt. I can't believe she didn't feel the same way about him that he felt about her. I'm sure his feelings were genuine. He poured his heart out in that letter we wrote. We were laughing so hard I thought I would choke. It was tough to tell her who had really sent the letter. We were afraid she would kick our butts.

6

Being Real Police

After working in the jail for almost five years, my name came up on rotation to roll out again, and I decided it was time to be a real police officer. I wanted to take part in car chases, get shot at, see naked crazy people, go to robbery-in-progress calls and family fights, and make dope arrests—all that exciting stuff. Yeah right. I've done some of that stuff, but if you're in this job because of what you've seen on TV, you'll be disappointed. Murders can't be solved in an hour (including commercials); most are never solved. I can't beat a man senseless with a phone book during questioning over a stolen lawn mower or a forged check. Cars rarely leave the road when going over hills during chases, with the light bars popping off and hanging by the wire. Rich, beautiful woman don't throw themselves at you, wanting to have sex or to marry you, although I have had ugly women offer sexual favors to keep from going to jail or to get out of a ticket. *Please, lady! I'm writing you up for a*

misdemeanor traffic offense. You're going to take the chance of
getting pregnant or I'm going to take the chance of you giving
me a disease? I don't think so.

Chases are one of the more exciting parts of the job. They get
the blood pumping. One night we had just finished responding
to a loud-party call and were heading back toward our territory
when another small agency in our county got into a chase. It was
one of the numerous small agencies on our radio system, and
we headed that way. Before the chase ended, it went through
half of the county and eight jurisdictions. The suspect rammed
two vehicles, one a private vehicle and one a police unit. When
we finally made the stop, we discovered the driver was a fifteen-
year-old kid. He and his two adult passengers were trying to
buy dope.

Because most police work consists of paperwork, we had to
get statements and do incident/offense reports, arrest reports,
and a tow-in report. In making the stop, we damaged a county
unit, and that meant more paperwork. I was fairly new to patrol
and wanted to hone my writing skills, so my statement began
something like this. "It was a cool late-summer, early-fall night
when suddenly the silence was broken by whoo whoo whoo." (I
was trying to describe the siren sound.) You can imagine how
the rest of the story went. I thought it was a good statement.
It took up a lot of paper and ink, and I thought that's what my
superiors were looking for.

Apparently not. The weekend relief sergeant read it, looked at me, and said, "Rob, we are going to go with your partner's statement." His was just a monotone, play-by-play statement that had no jazz or humor. It listed the route and the direction we took, naming the streets. Blah, blah. However, the sergeant liked my writing ability so much he made sure the regular sergeant was left a copy with a note that *this* was my statement. The regular sergeant, who had known me only a few weeks and who didn't have a great sense of humor, started reading. After a few seconds, he looked as if someone had hit him with a skillet. His jaw clenched and his hands shook. He looked at the older deputies in the room and asked, "Y'all didn't let him turn this s—t in, did you?" There was so much laughter in the room all the deputies had fifteen minutes added to their lives. This was only one of my many creative writing reports.

Here is what really happened.

The small-town officer (in an attempt to obtain revenue for his town) started the chase with a drug customer, who had dashed out of town without paying. The officer chased the truck to another small town, where the truck rammed a local police unit head-on. The truck continued onto Highway 78 where we got into the chase. We were third in line behind the truck. The small-town officer who initiated the chase dropped out, and we became second. Our agency's lead unit was a brand-new police car with a new color scheme that the sheriff had just approved, and the deputy driving it was afraid to get it scratched, so he pulled back and we became first. As we chased the truck, my partner and I pointed out spots of interest, including one of my dad's stores.

The offender sped through a red light just as a late-model Ford with a green light was entering the intersection. What a crash! This one was like the crashes on TV. The Ford lost its front end, and the offender's vehicle lost its front tire. This was helpful to us in the long run because with the tire gone each time the vehicle slowed to make a turn, the steel rim ground down on the pavement, releasing a shower of sparks. It also helped that the offender used his signal at each turn. Looking to end the chase after the civilian vehicle was wrecked, my partner sought to pull up to cut off the offender's escape route. The offender's vehicle pulled out, and we barely missed him. He crossed the railroad tracks just as the warning lights came on, with us right behind him.

Tiring of this chase and ready to end it, we discussed shooting out the tires. After all, we had two county-issued shotguns loaded with buckshot. Unfortunately they were both in the trunk of the car. My partner pulled beside the truck and just ahead to cut it off. The driver rammed us, but as he did, my partner cut hard into the truck, forcing it into a ditch. After a vehicle has been stopped, the occupants almost always bail and have to be chased down. We discussed our plan during the chase. The driver would chase the driver, and the passenger would chase the passenger.

Thanks to Murphy's law, things rarely go as planned. My door was pinned against the offender's vehicle and would not open. The offender's door wouldn't open either. As his two passengers bailed, I pulled my weapon on him and held him at gunpoint while I crawled out of my open window. I took him into custody, and everyone else had to chase down the passengers. We took them to jail and wrote a bunch of traffic tickets to go with other charges. I think I wrote the driver four myself, which is not the most I ever wrote to a driver at one time, but I'll write about that later.

7

Field Training

I still remember my first night out. My agency now has what is called a field training program, but when I rotated out of the jail you went to patrol, the sergeant put you with someone, and you learned that way. You might ride with up to five people a week and see things five different ways. You might have to ride for up to two years. I didn't but I know a lot of deputies who did. The first night out I didn't get sleepy, probably because of the excitement. After all, the sergeant put me with one of the best officers our sheriff's office has ever had. This guy was a legend, and I had heard about him while working in the jail, so I was ready for anything.

We got through with our glad-to-meet-yas, and he asked me what kind of equipment I had been assigned and told me what else I needed to get from the property room. He got me some blank reports and showed me the best way to arrange them in my clipboard. He showed me how to prewrite a ticket. (Include the information that doesn't change, such as my name and the court info.) After a while we loaded our gear into the car and off we went. We drove behind a large strip mall to make sure nobody had kicked in any back doors. He stopped the car, got out, and urinated. He pulled around the front, checking the windows to make sure they were intact. He stopped and bought a bargain soda out of a machine. Our conversation went something like this.

"Robbie, can you kill a man?" the deputy asked.

"If it means going home, yes," I told him.

"Good 'cause I've got four daughters, and it's you and me against the rest of these motherf——s tonight."

He then pulled up to an intersection, and as the light was triggered to turn red for cross traffic, a car went on through it. The deputy turned on the emergency lights, and the car pulled onto the shoulder of the four-lane road. He told me that he was going to approach the driver and that I should get out and stand beside the car but not go past our headlights. "If he shoots me, you shoot him," the deputy said. I said I would. I am so glad there was no loose gravel for him to slip on, because if he had I would probably have emptied a magazine full of 9 mm hollow points into the back windshield, thinking he had been shot. I was gripping my handgun so tightly it's a wonder I didn't crack the cylinder.

The stop went without a hitch. He issued a ticket and we were off again. We went to a grocery store that was open twenty-four hours, and he bought some lean pockets to microwave. He called an officer he knew who worked for one of the small-town agencies in our county. We went to his station, and I spent most of the rest of the shift listening to them tell war stories. He was a great guy, and I got other opportunities to work with him when we were both assigned to our detective division.

8

Good Girl, Lassie

I was going to ride with this same guy on night shift, and while we were at roll call we got a call from a woman saying her neighbor's dog had been shot and had died on her porch. We've been called when cows or horses enter the road, dogs bite people, and hamsters invade ladies' houses, and for other problems with animals, but usually they're live animals. To beat it all, the address where the call came from couldn't have been farther from where we were. The territory we were working was eighteen miles or more from our substation, and this woman lived at the opposite edge of that territory, almost into the next county. The territory was about twenty square miles.

I was still new to this patrol thing, so I said ten-four and prepared to go, but the other deputy nearly popped a cork. "What are we supposed to do with a f——g dead dog?" he asked. "We can't call animal control. This is a waste of our time." He was furious. We loaded our gear and away we went, with my partner raising Cain. It took us thirty-five to forty minutes to reach the address, and he had cooled down by the time we got there. When we arrived we saw a large dog (mixed shepherd type, about seventy-five pounds) dead as a hammer just beyond the top of the steps on the porch. We knocked and no one answered. We knocked again and still got no response. We had the dispatcher call the complainant, and the dispatcher told us the complainant said she'd gone to bed.

This rekindled my partner's fury. He repeated his rant and even called the sergeant on duty and had him call the lieutenant. We were told to try to contact the owner of the dog, but no one was home. After that we were told to move the dog off the complainant's porch. In my equipment bag I had a rope about fifteen feet long. I don't know why. I tried to think of anything I might need. Rope came to mind, and it was at the house when I packed my gear. The rope came in handy more than once, and this wasn't the last dead dog I would encounter. I got the rope and my partner tied it around the dog's neck.

The dog had been dead long enough to begin to get stiff, and it wasn't a small animal. After fighting to get the dog down the steps, my partner wasn't too happy. Then he started dragging it across the yard toward the neighbor's property. I probably didn't help matters with my witty banter. "You know if you call her by name, the dog will probably be more cooperative. Come on, Lassie. Come on, girl." I acted as if I heard the dog barking and said, "What's that, Lassie? Timmy fell in the well?" After dragging the dog about sixty yards, we left it on the edge of its owner's yard and took off, with my partner still fussing and cussing. I believe if he had gotten to the car before I did, he would have left me to walk back. Come on, Lassie. Come on, girl.

9

Freeze

One night I was riding with one of my chums, and we got a call to back up another unit at one of our high-class trailer parks. A man armed with a knife was chasing people. We got there first, which wasn't surprising, knowing the deputy who was working that territory. When we rolled into the park, we saw people running from a guy and pointing at him, saying, "That's him."

My partner was driving and pulled in closer to the guy to find out what was going on. I got out on the passenger side and the guy walked toward us. I saw he had a knife, but for some reason my partner was preoccupied with the complainants and didn't notice this at first. I pulled my weapon, pointed it at the guy, and yelled at him to freeze. I think I scared my partner as much as I did the guy with the knife. The man dropped the knife, and when it clattered on the pavement, my partner knew why I had gotten so loud. I commanded the guy to get on his knees, and in his intoxicated state he pretty much belly flopped to the pavement. Yeah, he went to jail. On the way out of the trailer park, we passed the deputy who was assigned the call. We kept on going to the jail. See ya.

10

Uh, We'd Better Go

I was working the evening shift and received a call to back up another unit on a robbery call. Our territories on some of our outlying beats are pretty large, so when we reached the business, the offender had made his getaway and had about a ten- to fifteen-minute head start on us. I got a vehicle/offender description. A white male armed with a sawed-off shotgun was driving a midseventies' station wagon, dark colored and with the back driver's-side window busted out. I checked the area while the other deputy gathered information from the clerk. One of the smaller agencies in the county got an anonymous call naming the person who committed the robbery. The agency had jailed this man, so there was a photo of him. *Great*, I thought. *Now we'll have a photo to include in a lineup.*

I headed off toward the agency, which was a short distance away, and was stopped at a red light on the main street just a half block from the office. Suddenly I spotted a white male at the wheel of a dark blue, late-seventies Ford station wagon with the driver's-side back window busted out. He was approaching from a side road and had the green light. Now this was around 1998. Other than a semitruck, this Brady Bunch wagon was probably the biggest vehicle on the road. How could I not see it? This was 98 percent luck, 2 percent skill. I fell in behind the vehicle and asked the dispatcher to send some backup my way. The driver was halfway through the little town, and I realized he was headed toward a part of the county I'd never worked and where I knew none of the roads. I chose to light him up and to try to stop him on my own.

I prepared for the chase that would surely ensue by tightening my seat belt. I turned on the emergency lights, but instead of flooring it, the driver immediately pulled over. As I yanked off my seat belt, I keyed my two-way mike to tell the dispatcher where I was. The driver opened his door. Since he hadn't run, I thought he was going to shoot it out with me. I expected to see the business end of the sawed-off shotgun the store clerk had just seen. I kicked my door open and yelled at the driver to stay in the car. I had gotten the drop on him by getting my gun out first. I ordered him to put his hands up. I hadn't experienced complete tunnel vision yet, and I was aware of two people on the sidewalk where we stopped. After I kicked the door open with my gun in my hand and yelled at him in my most commanding voice, one of them said to the other, "Uh, we'd better go."

No shotgun ever appeared, but the driver stuck his head and his hands out of the window. He was alone and I moved in closer, keeping the front end of the patrol car between us. I was just about to tell him to stay put when he said shakily, "I'll crawl out the window if you want me to." I thought for about half a second and told him to do that. The guy slithered out of that window like a snake. His hands never touched the door as he slid out onto the street. When I had him spread-eagle on the pavement, I commanded him to look away from me. I moved in and told him to put his hands behind his back. I cuffed him and was standing him up when the backup arrived. He was taken to the store for a lineup, and the clerk said he was the robber. I heard he later admitted to the robbery and claimed he threw the shotgun in a pond. I also heard his baby's mama was the anonymous caller. Arrests are easy when offenders comply. I believe while I was pointing that gun at him I could have yelled, "Do the hokey pokey," and he would have.

It's not as easy when they don't comply. One night I received a call about a small tan pickup being driven recklessly. This was a patrol request; the complainant didn't want to talk to the police but wanted someone to check the area. It was between three and four in the morning, and the area was pretty much vacant. I was patrolling two to three miles from the location of the call, and I saw a small tan pickup and a black car turn rapidly onto another road. The two vehicles then pulled side by side like they were racing. The black car pulled ahead of the pickup. I was behind the two, and I also pulled ahead of the tan truck. The black car didn't slow down, and it was weaving pretty badly.

I turned on the emergency lights, but the driver had no intention of stopping or couldn't see out the window. It was early on Super Bowl Sunday in 1996, and there was a heavy frost on the back window. I pulled alongside of the car so the driver could see the lights, and the vehicle slowed and finally stopped. I went to the driver's side and a white female rolled down the window. The pickup had fallen behind, but as I was talking to the woman the driver pulled up and stopped in the middle of the road. I went to the driver's side of the pickup, and a white male rolled down the window. The two were husband and wife, and in the short time I had talked with them I could tell they were both intoxicated. I got the husband out to do field sobriety tests, but he was uncooperative. I told him to put his hands on my car because he was under arrest. As I patted him down for weapons, he reached back and grabbed for my gun. I felt it start to come out of the holster and locked my arm around his and jerked him to the ground. The fight was on.

We were beside his wife's car and I saw her start to get out. I yelled at her to stay in the car. She briefly seemed to comply, but then she started to get out again. Because of this, I could not give her husband my full attention. I felt him starting to get away from me, so I reached back and hit him, thinking if he got away maybe he wouldn't be as interested in my gun. I don't think he was trying to get the gun to clean it for me. I later realized I had hit him in the eye and was still holding my

handcuffs at the time. He ended up with a nice shiner for the jail photo. Too bad. He ran off into the woods. At some point I managed to hit the orange Oscar Sierra button on my walkie-talkie radio. Other deputies knew I was not one to call for backup during DUI arrests. They knew the sky must be falling, and they headed my way.

When the man disappeared into the darkness, I didn't know whether he had a gun, so I waited for backup before looking for him. In the past K-9 officers had told me, "Watch where the suspect goes so we have a place to start the dog." I went to the wife's car and told her to get out because she was under arrest. She did. I handcuffed her and put her in the back of the patrol car. That was all! I didn't pat her down. I didn't have to. Her clothing was tight enough that I could pretty much see she didn't have any weapons. After she was in the car, her husband came walking out of the woods with his hands up. I cuffed him and put him in the back of the car with her.

Just before the first backup arrived, the adrenalin rush started to wear off, and I was standing about twenty feet behind the patrol unit so no one could see me. I was sucking wind like I couldn't get any. I had loosened the straps on my bullet-resistant vest because I felt like it was crushing me. I never found out why the man ran off into the woods, but I figure he was dumping dope. We found a stiletto-type knife or letter opener on the seat where his wife was sitting. I'm guessing she was trying to get out of the car during the fight to stick the pig. They both went to jail, and they both went to court. He fought his charges, including attempted murder. She pleaded guilty to her charges.

I thought that was the end of it. But in December of that year, just after the grand jury returned a true bill on the man's attempted murder charge, I was served with paperwork. The woman was suing me for an inappropriate search on the side of the road. In short she said I fondled her hoots and touched her Virginia. It took two and a half years, but every court threw out the suit. It seemed they believed me over them. But this suit probably bothered me more than having a razor put to my throat. I realized that even though I'd done nothing wrong, people could still bring false charges against me.

11

He's Got Two Fighting Him

More than one time the sheriff's office has had dispatchers come out and ride with patrol units. This helps each learn who's on the other end of the radio and helps dispatchers learn the territories beyond what's on the map. One night a dispatcher was at the substation, and either I drew the short straw (not knowing there was a drawing) or the sergeant was mad at me, because she rode with me. This dispatcher was later run off or fired from the sheriff's office. They had her on tape in the dispatch office bragging to someone about sitting at the sheriff's desk at night while no one was there and doing coke (not the soda). I guess she didn't realize all the phone calls were recorded.

There was a well-known barbecue place in my territory, and they always treated us well when we ate there. They kept the kitchen open late because they knew we didn't come to work until ten thirty at night. The sergeant suggested I take the dispatcher to have some barbecue. (Here's another police joke. If you're in law enforcement and eat barbecued pork, does that make you a cannibal?) After stuffing myself with barbecue, I rode down the hill to one of our local bars to start making rounds. The place was just beside a major highway between Birmingham and Memphis. As I pulled into the parking lot, I saw a white male and a black male urinating in the lot. Though they had just left the bar, they didn't bother to use the restrooms. I got out of the patrol car and posed the question I always ask when I catch folks doing this: "Where you fellows from?" When they answered, I asked, "Well, don't they have bathrooms there?"

I obtained ID from the white male first because he was closer. I told him he was under arrest and put one handcuff on him. The dance was on. I took him down to the ground, but he was struggling enough that I couldn't get the other cuff on. His buddy started toward us, and the belly full of barbecue started churning. I took out my walkie-talkie to call for another car, but the white guy tried to get out from under me. I popped him in the back to restrain him, and his buddy started toward me again. I yelled for him to stay back, and he complied. Then his friend tried to get up again. Pop. He was down again. I didn't realize until later that every time I popped him in the back, my walkie-talkie radio keyed up. I wonder if he had bruises on his back that said "Motorola."

This went on for several minutes before the coke queen picked up the radio mike in the car and said, "One of y'all might want to come up here. He's got two of them fighting him." *Thank you for calling*, I thought. I felt like I was going to puke on my half-cuffed prisoner by the time the first unit slid to a halt. It was an election day, and even though they lived in a county twenty miles away, both these guys swore they had voted for "my sheriff."

12

He Was Wearing a Uniform

We now have take-home cars but we didn't always. There was also a time when we didn't have take-home walkie-talkies. One morning I was heading home in my personal truck. I was in uniform but I didn't have a walkie-talkie. I had a cell phone (actually a bag phone). Shortly after leaving the substation I fell in behind a drunk driver. I knew he was drunk because he was driving north and south in the westbound lane. I knew it would be useless to call our dispatch office to have one of our guys try to stop him because deputies on the day shift usually drank coffee for the first hour and a half before they loaded their gear into the cars.

I'm not saying they were lazy. They had righteous reasoning for this. Our substation was on the inbound side of the highway going toward Birmingham, and in the mornings so many people were trying to get to work that it was nearly impossible to enter the flow of traffic. Then there was school traffic. And when drivers see marked patrol units, they respond by jamming on their brakes, so by staying off the highway, the deputies were preventing accidents and keeping the public safe. That's what they told me. So I called to have our dispatcher patch me to one of the smaller agencies to try to intercept the driver. We went through two agencies and couldn't get anyone, so I called my dispatcher again.

As I did this, the guy stopped on the shoulder of the highway. I stopped behind him. This is a four-lane highway and the main route between Birmingham and Memphis. This guy got out, went to the front of his truck, and started urinating. Dispatch told me a unit was en route, but I knew how long that would probably take, so I figured I'd try to delay the driver. I approached him just as he was finishing up. I told him I needed to see his ID, and when I got it, I asked my stock question, "Don't they have bathrooms where you're from?" I knew the answer to the question because this guy was from my town, and I had indoor plumbing. Besides, as it turned out, I knew him. Until this incident, his mother cut my wife's hair. He must have figured something was up and headed back to his truck. I thought this was a good time to make my move.

I told him he was under arrest. Though I was parked behind him with flashing lights on, I guess he didn't hear me or didn't believe me, because he continued walking toward his truck. I took hold of his arm, and he swung and sucker-punched me just below the right ear. This dazed me but I managed to keep my grip on him. I tried to give him a dose of pepper spray, but I couldn't get a good shot on him. Every time he tried to open the door, I swept his arm aside and pulled him away from it. He pushed me into the highway a couple of times, but luckily there was no traffic coming.

Suddenly a drunk chick rose up and opened the door. She must have been passed out on the seat beside him and realized he was gone. He managed to get close enough to grab the steering wheel, and I couldn't pull his hand loose. He started to drive away with the door still open. I let go because I didn't want him to drag me, and I wasn't going to jump in the back, because only an idiot gets into a vehicle knowing the driver is intoxicated. I got in my truck and followed him to observe his actions. I was never in pursuit. I was merely following him to advise the responding patrol unit where he was going and to document any traffic violations or other offenses he might commit.

He managed to get away before the patrol unit arrived, mainly because he was willing to drive like an idiot and I was not. However, I knew who he was because I had his license. When I got a person's ID, I would look at the name and then stick the ID in the big buckle of my gun belt. In Alabama if someone gets away after a traffic offense, police have one year to locate the person and to serve traffic tickets. I felt like I owed this guy at least five. I added charges that would call for warrants on him. I wrote out the tickets and figured I'd get a chance to serve them when he was picked up and jailed on the warrants. He must have guessed there would be charges because he turned himself in and made bond before I found out.

I knew I would still have a chance when the court date arrived, but as luck would have it, as I was driving to work one night, I spotted this guy headed my way on the highway. I told you I was charmed. I called dispatch and got a marked unit to stop him. The folks on the evening shift had a different philosophy from the ones on the day shift. I got my tickets signed. Before we went to court, this guy had his attorney call our internal affairs department to complain about me. The lieutenant in charge of internal affairs told the attorney he wasn't going to let him complain about a deputy for someone else. If his client wanted to complain, he could go through the proper channels. I never heard anything else about it. This is a tactic many use to try to have charges reduced or dropped.

When we went to court the guy wanted a hearing to fight the charges. I took the stand to present the case for the prosecution. After my testimony, he took the stand in his defense. He pleaded innocent to all charges and testified that he fought with me because he didn't know I was a police officer. When the assistant district attorney asked him if I showed him a badge or other identification, he replied in loud voice, "Well, he was wearing a uniform." When he said that, the judge just shook his head because the guy pretty much blew his own defense out of the water. The judge found him guilty. A deputy sitting next to me in court leaned over and said the only part of the defendant's testimony he knew was true was the claim that I had asked the guy whether they had bathrooms where he was from.

As I mentioned, this guy's mother cut my wife's hair. After I made the charges against him, I suggested she might want to seek out another stylist. My wife said she didn't think she would have to, but when I told her about the "I'm trying to kill you with my stares" look this woman was giving me in court, my wife thought it was probably best if she went to someone else. After all, my wife wouldn't be nearly as cute with her hair cut like mine (bald).

13

I Wish I Had Appointed an Attorney

There was this guy who thought he was a real bad ass. In fact, he was just an ass and only bad to his wife. We'd answered several domestic calls. He'd bang her around but she never wanted him charged. One night I was cruising around and saw them in the parking lot of a convenience store. He was giving it to her pretty good. I hadn't seen him hit her, but he was intoxicated. He was going to jail for public drunkenness. If I couldn't get him for domestic violence, she deserved one night of peace. I hooked him up and put him in the back of the patrol car, and she was glad.

On the way to the jail, he started raising Cain and cussing me. I didn't think much of it. After all, we're supposed to be immune to that type of abuse. I hit the record button on the micro-cassette recorder I always carry and let him talk. He decided he would fight the charge, and when the case went to court his wife was there in his defense. (This was true love.) They testified he wasn't drunk, and because she appeared in his defense, it looked like the judge would rule in his favor.

I advised the judge I had a recording of this guy. The judge said he'd like to hear it. I hit the play button and put the recorder on his bench. He listened to about fifteen seconds' worth and shut off the recorder. His appearance went from interest to anger. He told the guy if he wasn't intoxicated, he had the filthiest mouth he'd ever heard. The judge said he wished he had appointed a defense attorney so he could have given the guy the maximum jail time. He found him guilty and fined him $500 plus court costs. Fines for public drunkenness were generally $25–$75 plus court costs.

Following my usual custom when I finished with a case, I said, "Thank you, Your Honor." As I turned to leave, the wife said something under her breath that I could not make out but that the judge did. He roared, "This is a joke? You think this is a joke, young lady? I'll show you a joke. You're in contempt of my court." He ordered the bailiff to take her into custody. I don't know what happened to her, because I didn't stay in court. But I do know she later separated from her husband, and when he talked her into meeting with him about getting back together, he choked her to death and drove her body around all night in a car. He went home the next morning and called dispatch to report what he had done. He waited on his front steps and turned himself in when a deputy arrived.

14

I Gots to Protect Myself

One night I provided backup for one of my chums on a call about a black female walking down the middle of a road. Chum, as you probably know, is bait you throw out to attract sharks when you're trying to catch them. When we got to the scene, we found the woman was intoxicated. We arrested her, hooked her up, and put her in the back of the patrol car. My chum then took her to jail. Simple, huh?

Later at meal break my chum jokingly asked why I didn't take the knife from her. "Because I didn't find a knife," I said. I told him I stood by while he checked her. Why didn't he find it? I wanted to know. He then told me that when he got her to the jail, the female deputies searched her and she pulled out a steak knife point down from inside her vagina. He joked she would have had time to retrieve the knife and chop up a busload of nuns before I would have looked in "that thing." When they asked her at the jail why she had the knife there, she replied, "I gots to protect myself."

15

Hair Club for Men

One night one of my chums stopped a vehicle, and the driver turned out to be intoxicated. I asked the guy for general information for our reports. Anyone who knows me or who has seen me without my ball cap (which I call the poor man's toupee) knows I'm as bald as the day I was born. The judge who handled our traffic cases was also bald, but he seemed more sensitive about it than I was. Having made numerous DUI arrests, I had been before this judge on several occasions. As I was getting information from the guy in the back seat, he looked at me and said, "You need to call the Hair Club for Men." I replied, "I'm bald! Why didn't anyone tell me?"

This guy fought his DUI charge. Since I assisted in the arrest, I was put on the stand to testify. The defense attorney asked if there was anything I remembered his client saying on the roadside. Not knowing what the attorney was getting at, I replied, "Yeah. He said I needed to call the Hair Club for Men." The judge stood up, and raising his voice he said, "What? I don't think that was the answer the defense attorney was looking for." My response had sent the attorney backpedaling, but I was under oath and sworn to tell the truth. By the way, the guy was found guilty.

16

The Schoolmarm Outfit

One night as I sat doing paperwork just up from the businesses that entertained gentlemen at night (topless redneck bars), I received a call about a person down. Normally these calls resulted after people had too much to drink, and they got a free trip to spend the night in the county jail. The sheriff's office dispatch also said medics were on the way. I arrived in just a few seconds and saw the bar owner peeking out from behind the door and pointing at a white female lying on the ground nearby. I got out to check on her and saw probably the second-largest knot I had ever seen on a person. It was still growing as I stood there.

At just about the same time I heard tires sliding on the pavement and saw a small car racing toward me. I pointed my weapon at the idiot in the car as he stopped a few feet from me. He jumped out and started yelling. I quickly discovered he was intoxicated, hooked him up, and put him in the back of the patrol car just as medics and my backup arrived. He was ranting about the bar owner hitting his wife with a slapjack. This is generally a piece of leather with lead or another hard object sewed into the end. It fits easily in a pocket and can be deployed fairly quickly. I guessed this guy got into it with the bar owner, and his wife either tried to intervene to help hubby or just got too close.

She was being very uncooperative with the medics and was refusing treatment. She also didn't like the fact that her husband was in the back of my car. She got up and walked toward their car. After being told numerous times not to drive, she got behind the wheel and almost backed into four medics and a deputy. I had to arrest her. She resisted when I tried to retrieve her from the car, and I had to give her a sample of our chemical defense (pepper spray). I've seen this stuff work on people, but it really did the trick with her. Her eyes slammed shut and the river of snot started. It was like the stalactites you see hanging in caves. She calmed down, and the trip to the county jail was free of any more excitement.

When we got to the jail it was a different story. If I had multiple prisoners or a female prisoner, I would always have another deputy come out and walk them inside with me. Because I had a female prisoner this time, I requested a female deputy. She met us outside, and since my prisoner's eyes were still mostly shut, the deputy escorted her inside and to a chair near the drunk meter for a test. The woman was still calm as water in an out-of-order toilet. When prisoners enter the jail, the staff has them remove their personal property, locking it away until they are released. This includes jewelry. A female deputy with a long ponytail said, "Hon, you need to take your rings off." Without warning, my prisoner reached up and grabbed a handful of hair, and the fight was on. It took six or seven deputies to make her release the hair and to restrain her. After the battle was over I told my backup deputy, "If she had fought like that on the street, she would have kicked both our asses."

The woman fought the charges. When the case went to court she was almost unrecognizable. I've heard of people cleaning up for court, but that doesn't begin to describe how she looked. She was dressed like one of those schoolmarms in the old westerns. The only thing she lacked was a parasol. She claimed she had never been to a place like the strip club and went there that night with her husband only because it was her birthday. I always try to take my wife to a movie or to a nice restaurant on her birthday. If only I had known that women really want to visit strip joints for their birthdays. The woman went on and on about how she was heading for a church social that night but went in the wrong door, and then the evil villain tied her to the railroad tracks because he wanted the money she had raised to pay for organ transplants for two hundred orphans. At one point she became so breathless I thought she was going to get the vapors. I don't think the judge bought the story either. She was found guilty.

17

Ride Along Again!

Like the dispatchers, some of the young assistant district attorneys would come out and ride along with us. One night I got a call about a man being assaulted. One of the assistant district attorneys was riding along with one of my chums. Being a chum, he radioed to say he would back me up. He wasn't too far behind me, but as usual I got there pretty quickly. When I arrived I found a white male on his knees and pushed up against a concrete porch railing. Another white male was on top of him and was still beating him like a drum. I commanded him several times to release the man, but he was too preoccupied and ignored me. Not one to be ignored, I repeated my request, but this time I made sure he had reason to believe I was serious. He suddenly stopped beating the guy but was still choking him as he had been when I arrived.

I finished pulling him off the guy as my backup appeared. As I was doing this, I heard the assistant district attorney say, "I shouldn't be seeing this. I'll probably be handling this case." She worked in the district court where cases usually went first. Still, that wasn't the last time she came out with us.

18

Goober Boy

Occasionally the sheriff's office will have interns come out and ride. Generally these are criminal justice students. I nicknamed one kid who used to ride along with us Goober Boy only because I couldn't remember his name. I call him a kid because at the time I knew him he was just getting out of college. Since he had gone to college with one of our captain's sons, he got to come out more frequently than most interns. This kid was good at ball, but although he could probably have gone to the major leagues (I think he played some semipro), he wanted to become a police officer and eventually did. When he returned home he joined the force there, and I heard he became pretty good at it.

On the kid's first night out the sergeant put him with me. We sat in roll call and then loaded up the gear in the car and took off from the substation. We pulled out onto the highway, and after a half-mile we fell in behind a vehicle swerving all over the road. After stopping the vehicle and having the driver step out, I determined he was intoxicated. I hooked him up and took him to jail. Boom. After that, Goober Boy was hooked. I had never seen anybody who wanted to be a police officer more than he did—probably not even me. He rode with us again and again. I believe during college breaks, he came out every night. I often wondered if I would have wanted this job if I could play ball like he did. He was a great guy, and I hope if he's still policing he's safe.

19

Habitual Traffic Offender

One night I was working a traffic detail with one of my chums. We were set up in the middle of the highway and had not had any serious bites. We were just about to call it quits and go get a bite to eat when suddenly a car with one headlight broke the highway's darkness. We weren't having much luck with radar, so my chum said, "Let me write this guy a ticket for one headlight and we'll go eat." In Alabama equipment violations are nothing. You get the problem fixed within seventy-two hours, mail in a copy of the receipt, and it costs you nothing but the price of the bulb, which you needed anyway. My chum turned on his headlights and his emergency lights and put the car in gear, and as the guy passed us we heard him floor it. My partner was driving a newer car than the one I was driving, but for some reason it had never run that well.

At this time we all carried personal citizens band radios in our units. We would listen to the semitruck drivers yell about the drunks and would talk to each other so dispatch could hear. My partner called me and told me that he wouldn't be able to catch this driver and that I would have to slow him down. "No problem," said. "I'll get him." Why is it that every time I say something like that things don't turn out the way I expect? The car I was driving was really fast, but it had been wrecked when some drunk chick T-boned it on the interstate. However, the county doesn't throw anything away. The county shop fixed it. But the repair crew either didn't know the sway bar was bent or replaced it with a homemade one made from coat hangers. Even though it was fast, the car didn't handle worth a flip on curves.

I was on the driver right away on the highway, but then he took to the twisty side roads and I had to back off. My chum managed to catch up to us at this point. The driver wasn't from our area, so he didn't know where he was going. He made a lot of turns until he wound up on a main street in one of our towns. The street led back onto the highway. When we hit the highway he took off like a scalded dog. My car was fast, so I was on him quickly, but my chum again fell behind.

I saw my chance to get the driver. As he was approaching an eighteen-wheeler, I shot past him and my chum radioed the truck driver and asked him to slow down. When my partner caught up to us, I slowed down, let the truck pull away, and got in front of the guy's car.

My chum was to his left and I was in front, and we slowed down until we got to a spot we liked and stopped. It was a classic box-in move. When we had stopped the driver, we took him to jail for resisting arrest and for reckless endangerment. (He had two underage girls with him, and I'm sure their dads were thankful to us for saving their chastity that night.) He was found to have a suspended driver's license (Florida issue) for being a habitual traffic offender. I helped him maintain that status in Alabama by writing him eighteen traffic tickets.

If he had stopped, he would have been cited for an equipment violation and would probably have gotten a ticket for driving with a suspended license. The judge questioned the number of citations I wrote, but when I explained the driver's status in Florida he understood. I think he might have cut the driver a small break, which was fine because I think the guy got the point.

20

Nah, I Got Him

One night we got a call about a wooded area being on fire. I don't know about other sheriff's offices, but if somebody calls our office and says, "My neighbor is raking his leaves into my yard," we send a car. This turned out to be an unauthorized bonfire, and it was called in by a volunteer fire department, which was on the scene with a brush truck. The firefighters were on the road, and the fire was about a quarter-mile away up a goat trail on top of a hill. The fire department advised us that because of the dry weather there was a no-burn order. That gave us enough reason to make the fire starters put out the blaze.

We started up the hill, and over the CB my chum asked, "How are they going to put the fire out?" I replied, "With the cold beer they're drinking or they can urinate on it." When we reached the top of the hill, we were still about fifty yards away from the fire and could see a group of about twenty people. One guy (there's always one) jumped in a Nissan 4X4 pickup and took off toward the goat trail, heading through the woods. "You want me to go get him?" my chum asked. "Nah. I got him," I said. Once again, things would not go as I anticipated.

The goat trail turned into a path that even goats wouldn't take. The driver was in a 4X4 pickup built for this type of terrain, and I was in a vehicle built for the highway. However, I had one advantage over him: power. When he went slopping through the muck, I hit the gas and shot through the mire to avoid getting stuck. I fishtailed a few of times, once badly enough to take out some pine saplings, but I managed to keep him in sight. The goat trail eventually wound back to the road, and when we hit the pavement again, I shot past the guy, forcing him to stop. I discovered he was intoxicated in addition to being stupid. When the case went to court, he was fined for the traffic violations and charged for the damage done to the patrol unit by the pine saplings.

21

Magic Trick

One night I was circling through a parking lot and checking businesses when some idiot came flying into the lot, squealing his tires and doing fishtails. He did this with a marked patrol unit in plain sight. It's not like we try to hide our cars. These large white vehicles have green-and-gold stripes and a huge star on both sides. He was an idiot for another reason: once he sped into the lot and past me, he couldn't escape because there was no other way to exit the lot. I turned on the emergency lights and pulled up to block him.

As he finished doing a doughnut, he saw me and stopped his car, facing mine and racing his engine. I exited my unit and approached his vehicle. He gunned his engine, causing his vehicle to lurch toward me. I pointed my weapon at him. This idiot was accompanied by a front-seat passenger. Both got Oscar-Sierra looks on their faces. The passenger's hands shot up in the air, but the idiot jumped into the back seat and tried to hide. He turned out to be intoxicated. As I was getting him out of the back seat to hook him up, he asked what he was being arrested for. When I told him he was being charged with driving under the influence, he said, "I'm not the driver. I'm in the back seat." I guess he thought I blinked and didn't see him perform his magic trick. Idiot.

22

I'll Follow You Anywhere

One night just after I could ride solo, a call came over the radio saying a local police department was involved in a chase with a stolen Explorer but had lost sight of the vehicle. As luck would have it, I was close to where the vehicle was last seen—real close. About two seconds after the radio call, I came across a vehicle matching the description, including the tag. I turned on the emergency lights and the chase was on.

Chases are dangerous, but anybody who won't admit they're fun is probably an administrator. You usually zero in on the vehicle you're chasing and follow it anywhere. That's what I did this time. I chased the driver along several back roads, and I guess he decided he wasn't going to lose me. He took one road, and I thought he was heading back toward the highway when he took another road, which was a dead end. I don't know if he knew that, but when he got to the end he turned into a driveway, which looked like part of the road, and I followed. When we got to the other side of the house, I guessed he was heading back to the road, so I didn't follow. I pulled up to block his exit and he cut into me. I cut the patrol car into him to shut him down. He had already done the damage to my vehicle.

The three people in the vehicle bailed out. The two passengers got away, but I managed to snag the driver. When the lieutenant asked why I ended up in someone's yard, I told him I thought the driver was still on the road, so I followed. I hope he doesn't read this, because he's my lieutenant again.

23

Slow-Speed Chase

One night I was working traffic detail. (You're starting to see a pattern, aren't you?) I was with one of my chums when we received a radio call saying local police were involved in a slow-speed chase with a truck. We waited a few minutes and sure enough they were coming in our direction. They were in our county now, so we had jurisdiction. We pulled out. Other agencies had gotten involved, so we were third or fourth in line. The truck wasn't going that fast, but the driver kept weaving across both eastbound lanes of a four-lane highway. Nobody was ahead of him, and it seemed nobody wanted to try to get ahead of him. He had no intention of stopping, and I guess the police were going to follow him until he ran out of gas.

In my fast car, I shot past the two police department units involved in the chase, and my chum followed. He started around the driver on the right, but when the driver weaved toward him, my chum backed off and fell in behind. I kicked the pig (which is what I nicknamed my unit) and blew past the driver on the left, got in front, and slowed down. I knew what my chum in back was doing. When I reached a slow enough speed, I stopped. The driver was going to stop or rear end me. He stopped. We got out and the fight was on. It didn't last long. I determined that the driver was drunk and stupid. The other agency wanted him for revenue, so we let the officers have him. Sometimes assisting is just as much fun. And there is less paperwork.

24

Freeze Tag

One night I was riding with one of my chums, and we were at a redneck bar checking on a deputy from our shift who had a part-time job there. We were standing in the parking lot and heard the roar of a car engine coming up the highway. We looked up in time to see a blur of a car going by followed by the blur of a police car. We jumped in our car and took off just as we received a radio call reporting the chase. Great timing, huh? We hit the road but they were already way ahead of us. Another of our units happened to be a few miles up the road and joined the chase. It continued for about sixteen miles along a four-lane highway and then moved onto a residential road, which went through a small wooded area.

The road had a sharp elbow curve. Did I mention the road was not lit and the night was very dark? The driver was about an eighth of a mile from home, so he knew the road. We knew the road from working the area, but the police department officer didn't. He braked when he got to the curve but realized too late how sharp it was and shot off the road. At that point the shoulder dropped off twenty-five to thirty feet. Until then, he was in the lead with one of our units second. That unit moved up to lead. We were about thirty seconds behind. The other deputy later told us that when the first unit went off the road it looked like the woods had swallowed the vehicle. The first officer was lucky the area was so wooded because the vines in the trees slowed his fall enough that the only injury he sustained was to his drawers. He later told us that although he saw he wasn't going to make the curve, he thought that the area looked pretty level and that he would spin around a few times and pull back onto the road. Was he surprised!

The sheriff's office unit continued the pursuit and radioed that the car's engine had blown. The guy was probably less than a block from his house, so he continued on and pulled up in his yard. He jumped out, and when the two deputies approached him, he yelled, "You can't arrest me. I'm in my yard." Then he punched one of the deputies in the throat. I guess he thought this was a game of freeze tag and he had made it to base. We tagged him anyway, and he was allowed to thaw out in the county jail. In case you're wondering, it was determined he was intoxicated.

25

That's My Car

The intern who went by the proud nickname Goober Boy (at this point I should call him a mascot) developed a bad habit after he started riding with us. He used to hang his car keys on the calendar at the substation because he didn't want to risk losing them if he got out of our vehicle. I guess he didn't know police tend to play practical jokes if given a smidgen of an opportunity. One night he was riding with me, trolling for drunk drivers on a main highway, when I saw a vehicle in the rearview mirror approaching pretty quickly. When it passed us, I picked up speed to pace the driver for a speeding ticket. If you pass a marked unit, I figure you're trying to flag me down to say, "I want a ticket."

About this time Goober Boy yelled, "That's my car." The vehicle that passed us was a white Chevy four-door, so I told him, "You drive a pickup." But he replied, "No, I traded with a buddy for the weekend." Being the suspicious type, I turned on the emergency lights to stop the car. Out of habit I also turned on the spotlight to light up the car's passenger compartment. The driver was wearing a hooded sweatshirt and kept pulling it over his head when it slipped. That was flag number one. Goober Boy freaking out was flag number two. The fact that I had never seen him in this type of car was flag number three. I thought he was trying to set me up for a joke, so I didn't get excited and didn't call in a pursuit. I called dispatch and said I was behind a vehicle that was refusing to stop.

Another flag was the direction the vehicle was being driven. Our substation was about two miles outside of Birmingham. So the driver could go to a city with three interstates running through it and pretty much disappear, but he was going twenty miles in the opposite direction. Something wasn't right.

The driver continued on for another half-mile and stopped completely off the road. We got out and could hear laughter coming from the car. Goober Boy, still freaking out and not in on the joke, raced up to the vehicle. A deputy had taken Goober Boy's keys and had gone trolling for us while we were trolling for drunk drivers. The joke was supposed to be on both of us. It was a funny prank, but Goober Boy seemed a bit upset at first. As I said, he developed a bad habit when he started riding with us.

26

Yeah, It'll Move

On another night I had Goober Boy riding with me on patrol. We were cruising along a small two-lane country road checking the area when I saw something in the middle of our lane. I saw a pair of eyes light up in the headlights. As we got closer, I could see a pretty big raccoon, and he was after something in the road.

"What are you going to do?" Goober Boy asked.

"It'll move," I said.

As we drew nearer, he asked, "You sure?"

"Yeah, it'll run," I said as I reached down and bumped the siren a few times. But this thing was defiant and stood its ground, continuing to paw at the road. I turned the siren on constant, still expecting the raccoon to run from the road. It didn't. I now know why raccoons aren't considered good pets. They're stupid. This thing stood pawing the pavement and looked up again just in time to disappear beneath the bow tie on our Chevrolet. I didn't know if the raccoon was badly hurt or hurt at all. I'd seen dogs get nailed like this, roll out from the back of a vehicle, and run off.

I stopped and went back to check on the creature. I would like to say no animals were harmed during the writing of this book, but I can't. I used a large stick to push the remains out of the road so other animals wouldn't risk the same fate for a meal. I wondered why the raccoon was willing to give up its life. What was this fatal attraction? I went back to the spot in the road. Someone had thrown out a half-eaten candy bar. I'm not going to say what kind it was, but I will say the raccoon died satisfied.

27

Boyfriend/Girlfriend Thing

There are a lot of firsts you remember when you become a police officer. I remember my first DUI arrest and my first solo car stop, and I can still take you to the locations where I made them. I remember my first solo car theft/recovery report, which I made just after ending my rookie period and being turned loose. I got a call to go to a cheesy motel (which we refer to as a dope and poke) about a stolen car. A dope and poke is a motel where you can rent a room by the hour, and you wouldn't want your wife or the pastor of your church to find your car parked out front. I talked to the victim, who gave me a description of the car and of the woman who took it. He knew her only by her nickname and admitted she was a prostitute.

After taking the information, I relayed it to dispatch, which entered the vehicle as stolen and issued a BOLO (be on the lookout) to surrounding agencies. I also checked the general area. After coming up empty, I continued my patrol duties. I had about an hour left in my shift before going home, but it was still dark out. A vehicle approached me with bright lights on. I flashed my headlights, but the driver did not dim the lights. I flashed my red-and-blue overhead lights, but the driver still did not dim the lights. I went after the vehicle to write a traffic citation. After all, if you ignore all the pretty lights the sheriff puts on his cars, I figure you're flagging me down because you want a ticket.

As I caught up to the vehicle I saw it was the same make and color as the one reported stolen just a few hours before. When I turned on the emergency lights to stop the car, I noticed it also had the same tag number. When I keyed the microphone to call in the stop, my voice was bursting with pride. This didn't last. A couple of backup cars arrived along with the shift sergeant and the lieutenant. The lieutenant said that we (meaning me) would handle this and that a detective shouldn't be called.

I contacted the victim. (I have to call him that because he made the theft report.) He said he wanted the girl to go to jail. I told him to meet me later that morning at the district attorney's office to sign the warrant. We released his car to him. I took the prostitute to the county jail. She wailed all the way, claiming that we had made a mistake and that the guy had said she could use the car. She repeatedly called him by his first name (and it wasn't John), which was a clue.

Our shift ended at six thirty in the morning, and the DA's office didn't open until eight. The assistant DAs usually didn't arrive until nine o'clock to screen warrants. The screening process works like this. An officer goes to the DA's office and waits in line for a clerk to type up the facts as he presents them. Then the officer waits in another line to tell an assistant DA the facts. The assistant DA types up a synopsis of the facts in preparation for a court appearance. Then the assistant DA calls the victim into the office to get some facts and to make sure the victim wants to prosecute. When all the paperwork is finished, the officer takes the victim up to a magistrate. The victim swears to the truth of the charges in front of the magistrate and signs the warrant in the magistrate's presence. This process takes an hour and a half to three hours.

The victim showed up at the DA's office. I waited for a clerk. Then I waited for an assistant DA. Then the victim talked with the assistant DA and left. I talked with the assistant DA, and he told me the victim didn't want to prosecute the prostitute because this was just a boyfriend/girlfriend thing. She had stayed out too long with his car, and he had made the complaint to get back at her. No big deal, right? I'd been up since about three in the afternoon the previous day, and it was now about eleven in the morning. I was so aggravated I knew I probably wouldn't get any decent sleep for the shift coming up. I went to the magistrate and signed a complaint against the guy for filing a false report. This incident happened late in the year, so we waited until ten minutes to midnight on Christmas Eve to

79

knock on his door and serve the warrant. We weren't allowed to knock on doors and serve warrants after midnight. That was our sheriff's order. I was looking for a fat guy in a red suit to take to jail that night, but this guy worked out just fine for me.

28

I Just Wanted to Say Thanks

One night I was cruising along when the dispatcher contacted me about a call from someone reporting trouble at a residence next door. These calls are usually bogus, but this one turned out to have some meat to it. The call came from a mobile home park. In the South we call them trailer parks, but some people aren't familiar with that term. In most mobile home parks down here, the lots are separated by fifty feet or less. The caller said the man next door was beating his wife and son. She was watching this happen, and the dispatcher kept her on the line. The caller said that the man had just come home and appeared to be drunk and that after beating his wife, he woke up his son and beat him. The woman said all the lights were on and she could see everything.

As usual, because the territory was so big, any backup units were so far out that I got there ahead of them. I didn't know at the time that the caller was still on the phone with the dispatcher, giving a play-by-play. I got out of the car and heard a woman scream. The front door of the trailer was open. Normally on domestic calls I wait for backup. I've always stuck to this rule, as we're supposed to do. But when I heard that awful scream I didn't. I knocked and announced, "Sheriff's office." I thought I heard someone say, "Come in." Because I did not know the situation, I unholstered my weapon. Then I started down the hall toward the screaming.

There was no one in the kitchen or the living room, which were undisturbed. I took a look in the bedroom and saw a disturbing sight. A small-framed woman was backed as far as she could get into one corner, screaming and covering herself. A much larger man (taller than I but thinner) had his back toward me and was beating a small-framed boy. Because of his size, I thought the boy was about eight years old, but it turned out he was eleven. The man was beating him with a stick about half the length of a walking cane. This stick was a piece of furniture he had broken during his rampage. When he got home, the man had awakened the boy just to beat him. The boy was in bed, shielding himself with his arms. I later learned the boy was the man's stepson.

When the man raised the stick for another blow, I thought it was a good time to get his attention. I had repeatedly commanded him to stop. I took one step into the room and planted my right Danner boot in his ass. He had knocked down the window blind, and the window was open or busted out, which gave the witness an even better view. If I had aimed my kick just right, I would have knocked him out the window. Instead he bounced off the wall and fell to the floor. This idiot jumped to his feet and raised the stick as if he was going to charge and hit whomever did this to him. He stopped when he saw the business end of my weapon. The look on my face probably was another slight deterrent. I told him to come for me, but he dropped the stick. I ordered him to face away from me and to get on his knees. I cuffed him and headed off to the patrol car, pushing him back the way I came.

The guy started whining about how he was messed up by the war and that's what made him do this. I'll admit that after seeing what I saw in that room, I went off on him a bit. When I got to the edge of the porch, I let him go. His lost his footing, and his momentum took him down the steps. That was probably the worst he got out of the whole deal. I had him up and in the back of the car before the medics and the first backup arrived. The woman was beaten so badly she had a knot on her face. When I interviewed her, I asked if it was a deformity or if her husband had done that to her. I knew of no other way to find out. He had also kicked her with the pointed toes of the cowboy boots he was wearing.

A robbery/homicide detective was called out because of the injuries. When he told me at the hospital he wasn't going to the assault scene, I was shocked. But I shouldn't have been surprised, considering previous calls he had been on. The detective said this was true love, and the woman would probably want to drop the charges when the case went to court. He was right. She sat on the defense side, giving me those if-looks-could-kill stares. The state took her two children because she allowed her husband to return home when he got out of jail.

That morning before I left the hospital to head home, I checked on the stepson. He was up on a gurney, partly covered. He looked at me and said, "You're the one that came in and got my stepdad, aren't you?" There was no denying it, and the next thing I expected to hear was what a bastard I was because I had taken his stepdad to jail. Instead something happened that I can't talk about without becoming emotional. Even while writing this, I still get choked up. He pulled his hand out from under the sheet, stuck it out to me, and said, "I just wanted to say thanks." Only this and the memory of my daughter's first steps and words still cause me to choke up. When I got home I told my wife what had happened. I could win the lottery or receive an officer of the year award, and it wouldn't mean as much as the handshake and thank-you from that boy.

Before I left the mobile home park I went to the caller's residence and viewed the scene from her vantage point. The view was so clear I might have been sitting in my living room watching a movie on television. I got an audiocassette of the 911 call. Some guys get copies of car chases they're involved in, but I never did. I pull this one out and listen to it every now and then. The cassette gives a play-by-play that goes something like this.

Dispatcher: 911. Do you have an emergency?

Caller: A man is beating his wife next door.

The address is verified and I'm dispatched. The caller is very emotional as she describes what is happening. The dispatcher is talking to her, and the caller says she sees a car pull up (mine). She says a deputy is going to the door and he's going in alone. "I see him in the room and he sees what's going on," the caller says. "The man is on the floor, and the deputy has got him in custody. He's leading him out the door. What? The man just threw himself on the ground. If he tries to say the deputy abused him, I'll go to court and say he did that to himself. The deputy's got him in the back of the car now, and I see other cars coming up."

I've often felt as if I owed that caller flowers or candy. You can't ask for a better caller. Oh yeah, I screened the warrants for the assaults against the mother and the stepson without the detective's assistance. He knew she wouldn't prosecute. She wanted to drop the charges against her husband for her injuries, but the state wouldn't let her drop the one brought against him on behalf of her son.

29

Don't Hurt My Baby

I am concerned about some of the drugs people manufacture. The kinds that are grown are bad, but there is consistency in them. Seeds are planted and they grow. The soil may vary, but there's not much difference in the product. When the stuff is made from recipes, you don't know what you're getting. If I get a recipe on the internet or by word of mouth and I'm not satisfied with it, I tweak it by putting in more of this or less of that. I'll jazz it up. If you don't like my recipe, you'll do the same but with different ingredients. You never know for sure what you're getting. Here's an example of this.

One night we got a call about a domestic situation. Dispatch sent a backup unit, but one of my chums was close and decided he would join us. I'm five eight and a half (I relish that half), and at the time I was about 215 pounds. My chum was five nine and about 225 pounds. We were working out at the gym because he was getting in shape to try out for the SWAT team. Neither of us was Mr. Universe, but we weren't wimps either. The backup deputy was at least six three and about 270 pounds. When we arrived mama and daddy were with Junior and his baby sister. The model American family, huh?

Mama and daddy called because Junior was acting strange. No physical violence had taken place—no pushing, hitting, or cursing. Junior had done nothing that would warrant taking him to jail. He was just acting strange and talking out of character. Junior was acting this way because he had taken bad bathtub acid or something similar at a party. And Junior was a pretty good size fellow, about the size of my chum. But we had no reason to arrest him, and if he had behaved for thirty seconds longer, we would have been gone and he could have gone to bed and slept it off.

We had almost finished taking information for the report. Junior was sitting at the dining room table talking to the pretend people on his shoulders when without warning he jumped up with both arms extended and hands open and shoved his father. Daddy was smaller than Junior and tumbled back. My chum and I reached for Junior to hook him up. The fight was on with superman. Whatever Junior had taken had him feeling no pain and had given him super strength. All three of us were on the floor trying to get him handcuffed, but we weren't succeeding. I decided that this was a losing battle and that one of us was about to get hurt or worse. I was considering stepping up force a notch to keep this from happening when mama screamed,

"Don't hurt my baby." I felt like screaming back, "Lady, I'm about to kill your baby," but I didn't and somehow we managed to get the cuffs on Junior. We got him up and took him out to the car. It took all three of us to get him in the back. He was still fighting and talking with the demons or the angels he kept seeing. When we got him in and closed the door, the backup deputy said, "I'll follow you down to the jail."

About a quarter-mile from the house, Junior rolled over on his back. When we got him in the car he had settled on his stomach, and I thought he wouldn't be as much trouble that way. When he got on his back he started kicking the roof of the car. I'd had prisoners kick the windows and the protective screen, but this was a first. We were on a back road and it was late at night, so I stopped in the middle of the road. I knew there would be no traffic coming by. I saw that when Junior kicked the roof, he had separated it from the back windshield. There was a gap in the rubber seal. We opened both rear doors and told him to stop, but he would only kick at the backup deputy. He was at Junior's feet and I was at his head. After seeing he was going to cause permanent damage to the patrol unit, we had to take steps to make him stop.

Enter Lassie's rope. I didn't have leg irons, and even if I did he would still have been able to kick because he was kicking with both feet. The backup deputy took the rope and tried to tie his feet, but Junior kept kicking him. I knew that to get him tied the kicking had to stop. For this to happen, we would have to distract him or get his attention. He was wearing a pair of cutoff sweatpants, so I reached in the back seat and grabbed a handful of the family jewels. He went limp. It's amazing that even when people are seeing angels or demons a simple act like this can get their attention. "Are you going to stop kicking that deputy?" I asked Junior. "Yes sir," he answered in a meek voice. I held him until the backup looped the rope around his feet and through the chain of the handcuffs. It was sort of a rodeo move. But when I turned Junior loose, it was like the bull had come out of the shoot again.

I called the jail when we got close to have a couple of deputies step outside to help us get him out. It took three of us to do it. Five deputies, a sergeant, and a weasel excuse for a lieutenant came out to give us a hand. The weasel looked at Junior, asked what was wrong with him, and refused to accept him until he went to the county hospital. I closed the door, and off to the county hospital we went, Junior and I with the backup deputy trailing behind. I had to take Junior to the hospital, but I couldn't make him accept treatment. It was his right to refuse, and I made sure he knew the place where we were going was probably crawling with those demons or angels he was seeing. There was a possibility one would come out to get him when we arrived. The backup deputy went inside to get a nurse while I explained he didn't have to stay.

The nurse came out, and I asked him if he wanted to be treated by this lady. He had been quiet, but he screamed, "No, no. Get away, demon," at the top of his lungs. I closed the door as the nurse handed me a clipboard to sign the refusal form for him.

89

She shook her head and walked back into the hospital like we had staged the scene. We returned to the county jail with our paperwork in hand. Hey, the jail can't refuse to send a prisoner to the hospital, but when you have the prisoner's signed refusal it's a free ticket back in.

The same five deputies, the sergeant, and the weasel lieutenant returned to get Junior out of the car. The weasel looked at Junior and said, "Untie him." I tried to tell him he might want to wait until Junior was out before he did that, but he wouldn't listen. *As you wish*, I thought. One of the deputies started untying the Lassie rope (Junior's wriggling had already added some slack), and when it got loose enough, Junior started kicking again. The weasel had stuck his head into the back of the car to help Junior out and received a stout kick as his reward. It took all seven of them to get Junior out after his feet were loose. I just stood back and watched. I felt like I had a free ticket to the show (the signed refusal slip). They ended up carrying him down the hall to the booking area and the holding cells with that Lassie rope trailing about ten feet behind. If only he could have held back those demons for thirty more seconds.

30

You Always Remember Your First

Here is another first I will never forget. One evening I had just left the jail after dropping off what I thought was the nightly drunk. As I was heading northbound on the interstate back to my territory, I fell behind a vehicle driving east/west in the northbound lanes. I stopped the driver and determined he was intoxicated. I hooked him up and put him in the back of the patrol car to take him to the jail. I called for a tow truck, and while it was on the way I began to fill out a pull-in, a form used to list info on the items inside the vehicle. I opened the console and found four or five small crème-colored pieces of crack cocaine. I froze. Was this really what I thought it was? Cool.

I had noticed empty beer cans on the back floor of the little car. A couple were mashed down in the middle, but I thought nothing of it. After discovering the crack cocaine, I called a more senior deputy who had worked dope cases in the past. When he got there he told me how dopers would flatten a can and poke holes in it to create a crack pipe. That way if they were able to dump the dope but got patted down they wouldn't have a paraphernalia (pipe) charge against them. Who would think twice about a flattened beer can? The suspect didn't get the chance to dump the dope. I sent it off and the results came back positive for cocaine. You always remember your first.

31

"Oh" Was All He Said

One night after bringing in the inevitable drunk and leaving the jail, I was heading north on the interstate, returning to my territory. I came upon a pickup truck that stood out to me because it was stopped. But the truck had not broken down. The driver was seated inside with the engine running, the truck in gear, and his foot on the brake. Another thing that stood out was that the truck was in the road. Before he passed out, the driver managed to get the passenger-side wheels on the fog line on the shoulder of the interstate. The fog line is the white line on the right side of the road.

I was able to get the truck in park and to awaken the driver. He was intoxicated, so I hooked him up to take him to the jail. As I was leading him to the patrol car, he asked, "What did you stop me for anyway?" I turned him around and showed him his pickup parked on the interstate. "Oh" was all he said.

The defense attorney approached me in court and said, "Deputy, can I talk to you about this case?" The assistant district attorney had told him he could ask to speak to me. In Alabama if you're in physical control of an operable vehicle, whether it's parked or going down the road, you can be jailed for DUI. But police usually need a reason to stop a vehicle— reckless driving or speeding, for example. However, I had jailed this driver only for DUI. There was nothing else to bargain away, a practice our DA's office is so famous for. The defense attorney thought he would have an easy win because of this. He thought this was a probable cause stop until he asked me what had alerted me to his client. What probable cause did I have to stop him? I pointed to my arrest report and told him his client's pickup was parked on the interstate. He didn't say much else. He spoke with his client and they pleaded guilty. The case didn't go to trial.

One of our dispatchers once told me that whenever I stopped a car he reached up and time-stamped a dispatch card. Now, whenever our dispatch office receives a call and it's typed into the computer, it's automatically assigned a dispatch number. At the time that wasn't the case. You called in for a dispatch number when you made an arrest. The dispatcher had to stamp a card to get a number. Generally the dispatcher didn't stamp a card on every traffic stop. He avoided doing this because if a deputy didn't call for a number for an arrest, the card and the number would have to be set aside until a number was required. But this dispatcher told me that whenever I made a traffic stop he went ahead and stamped a card because more than likely I would be calling for a number.

32

The Stagger-against-the-Deputy Test

Another first I can't forget is my first DUI arrest. I was still a rookie and was riding with a deputy as we passed a redneck bar. Suddenly an older-model Chevrolet Camaro came out of the parking lot at a high speed. We managed to stop the driver and spoke to him to determine why he was in such a hurry and whether he was intoxicated. I explained the field test I wanted him to perform, but he could only stagger toward me. If I had let him, he would have staggered against me. We determined he was intoxicated.

This is one reason I'm not a fan of field sobriety tests. If you're intoxicated enough that I can smell alcohol on your breath, you're probably intoxicated enough to go to jail. I shouldn't have to try to do balance tests on you and take the chance that you'll stumble out in front of a semitractor and get yourself flattened. Then your family would sue me for everything I don't have—like that $15 million I was sued for in 1996. It would take years of extra jobs and overtime to pay that amount.

This guy fought the charge in court, and his attorney wanted to argue that there was no probable cause for the stop. I guess flying out of a redneck bar parking lot onto a four-lane US highway in front of a sheriff's patrol unit and other vehicles is not cause enough to be stopped. He also wanted to argue that no field tests were done, but I testified that the driver almost staggered against me. This went on until the judge shut him down. The driver had failed the stagger-against-the-deputy field test.

He was found guilty.

33

PACT Fund

I'm sure a lot of you will find this hard to believe, but it is possible to arrest the wrong person. I don't mean you pick up an innocent person by mistake. I mean you arrest someone "they" don't want you to arrest. It may be someone who knows someone or someone who is someone. One night I assisted one of our units on a traffic accident. There were no injuries, but both driver and passenger were extremely intoxicated. Both were hooked up, and I made the offer to the two deputies in the other unit to transport both to the county jail. "Nah, buddy," one deputy told me. "You take the passenger and we'll take the driver."

Usually it would make sense for them to take the driver if they were going to charge him with DUI, but we didn't have a witness to put either person behind the wheel. Without such a witness, it was impossible to make a DUI charge. It was like the vehicle magically appeared. They were both going to the jail for public drunkenness. Besides, a deputy in the other car was milking the call for overtime. We headed for the jail, and while we were on the way my guy decided to get talkative.

"Call John Bender," he said. *Okay*, I thought. *I'll play your silly game.*

"Who is John Bender?" I asked.

"He's head of the PACT fund," the guy said.

"What's the PACT fund?" I asked.

"We give money to the PACT fund each payday," he said. "The PACT fund gives money to the sheriff and the judges to keep us out of trouble like this." (It wasn't working too well for him.) "If you call John Bender he'll tell you to turn around and take me home." Wrong.

We made it to the jail and I took my guy in first. As they were unhooking him, I looked up to see the other deputies coming around the corner. Their guy had a large wet stain on the front of his shirt. He had puked all over his shirt and inside their car. The car I was driving had a hard plastic insert inside of it. You placed this insert in the back seat, protecting it from such incidents. The other unit did not have the insert. The plastic insert also had drain holes, and if something like this happened you sprayed it with a hose. You couldn't do that with a regular seat. If the deputy hadn't been milking the overtime, the guy would have puked in the car I was driving. You know John Bender never called me about the case. I guess the PACT fund wasn't all it was cracked up to be.

34

Selective Prosecution

One night my chum and I were running radar on one of our unlicensed raceways and clocked a driver going well over the posted speed suggestion. We stopped this driver and determined that he was intoxicated and that he was under twenty-one, the legal drinking age. I hooked him up, and my chum did the pull-in for the vehicle and waited for the wrecker to tow. About halfway to the jail the guy in the back seat started telling me to call the sheriff. Now people often tell you this, thinking it might help them avoid jail. I've heard stories about how people make a phone call as soon as they arrive at the jail and about how the sheriff calls and says, "Let him out. I'll take responsibility. He's my gardener." And it didn't matter if the person was drunk.

But this guy called the sheriff by his name, as if he knew him. And this guy was nineteen (a kid) while the sheriff was about seventy. I assured him the sheriff was probably happily in his bed asleep and didn't want to be disturbed. But he kept insisting I call. Nothing clicked until I pulled the kid's license out of my belt buckle and started thinking about his name. Well, I never said I was the brightest bulb on the porch, but finally the bulb lit up. This kid had the same first and last name as our chief deputy. Could it be? Yes. This kid's dad also worked for us as a deputy. Nepotism? Nah.

I could have called the sheriff or the kid's old granddad (a brand he seemed familiar with) or even his dad. But I wouldn't have been doing anybody a favor. In fact, I knew this kid had been caught multiple times before and was taken home or had somebody called. Did he learn then? At the time it didn't matter to me. It still doesn't. I don't believe in selective prosecution. I will cut breaks on minor things, but drinking and driving is not one of them. You'll know why later. It doesn't matter if you're a bank president or a chief deputy's grandson. If you're drinking and driving you go to jail. Later when we were eating, my chum asked me, "Didn't you know who he was when you stopped him?" I said that I didn't until we were almost at the jail but that it shouldn't matter. "Okay," he said. "I guess you aren't that much into promotion."

35

Let There Be Lights

Working the night shift, I had just finished clearing a wreck and had found a flat spot to complete the paperwork and to do the diagram on the report. (Unlike officers in most nearby agencies, we have to file our reports when our shift ends.) Suddenly I heard one of our cars calling in a chase. This deputy could drive. You didn't want him running after you, because you couldn't lose him no matter what you did. It was also hard to keep up with him on a hot call.

One of the small-town agencies started this chase. An officer made a stop, and the driver tried to get away, dragging him. Another officer started chasing the vehicle, and they wound up outside the town limits. The deputy was getting coffee at a convenience store, and they went zipping by as he was about to pour a cup. (He later told me he was standing in the store and had just lifted the coffeepot when he saw an older-model

Dodge go flying by at about warp two. *This can't be good*, he thought. About half a second later the small-town cop followed. The deputy jumped in the car and away he went.)

The road on which the chase was taking place led toward me. There was only one road the driver could take to go back toward town, and when he passed that, we had him. I had to make it to the crossroads before they did. The deputy who radioed in the chase later told me when he heard my voice on the other end he knew we had him. It was my normal night off but I was working overtime. I got to the crossroads before they did but just barely.

I did something that one time that I'll probably never do again. I pulled up in the darkness about a quarter-mile from the crossroads on the narrow two-lane road and turned off all my lights. I know it was a stupid move. When I saw the headlights of the vehicle being chased, I hit every light on the unit. Let there be lights. The guy had been running for about fifteen miles down this dark, curvy two-lane road with a local cop behind him, and just before they reached my location the other sheriff's unit had caught up to the chase. The driver probably thought he was going to get away, and then he saw me. Not only did I surprise him but the small-town officer and the other deputy.

When the driver saw me, he swerved into a yard but got stuck off the road and tried to bail out. The small-town officer stopped her vehicle at his door so he couldn't open it. He bailed out on the passenger side, and that gave us time to get to him. The fight was on. He was a big guy and on two types of illegal dope, as he later admitted. It took all three of us to get him down and hooked up to go to jail.

36

He's Running

Some of the best times I had while working with the sheriff's office came when I was a field training officer. In this role, I worked with a deputy trainee (a rookie) who had been assigned to the jail for several years. It was our job as FTOs to teach trainees what to do on the road working patrol. I must have done something right or had a lot of people fooled because I had deputies assigned to the jail and waiting to come to patrol ask to ride with me. The rookies also told me they enjoyed riding with me, and I believe they were serious. While I was working this assignment, I still enjoyed my regular duties. I hadn't reached the burnout stage, and the training work had helped me find my spark again.

When the first trainee riding with me showed up at the station, I had not been told I was getting him. This wasn't uncommon. When he reported to me, he had just finished his first phase of training on the evening shift, and here I was on the night shift. He had to work a double shift so his time in would count. I asked how long he had been awake. He said since eight or nine that morning. It was ten thirty at night, and he had to be with me until six thirty in the morning. It was a Friday night, and since I would have him for two nights before our time off, I figured I would drive the first two to get to know him and to show him how I wanted him to drive. When we returned to work, I would put him behind the wheel and tell him not to hurt me.

As we rode, I explained that our job on the night shift mostly involved car burglaries (this is what I was told as a rookie) and that if we got a chance to work some traffic that was fine too. Maybe we would catch some drunk drivers. The night was uneventful. We stopped a few cars, wrote some tickets, and rode around checking businesses to make sure they hadn't been broken into. About a quarter to five I told him we would make a final pass at our businesses and would return to the substation. I would do my paperwork on him and let him go home a little bit early.

It didn't happen. On our beat there was a burger place with a twenty-four-hour drive-through. We were circling the parking lot, checking on the clerks to make sure everybody was okay. As we entered the lot, we saw something that looked a bit out of place. A vehicle was parked somewhat askew. It looked like it had pulled up from the side road to use the drive-through. When a vehicle already in the drive-through pulled away, our suspect vehicle didn't move up. An employee cleaning up the lot walked by and stared at the car. There was plenty of room between the vehicle and the building, so we circled around to see what was up. Someone was in the driver's seat. The employee said he didn't know him. I looked at the trainee and said, "Let's find out what's with this guy." The vehicle was running and in gear. The driver was passed out with his foot on the brake. As we got out, another unit arrived as backup. Knocking on the window, we got no response. The backup deputy saw a gun holster in the pocket behind the passenger-side back seat, so we were extra alert.

The driver's door was unlocked, so I opened it. After several minutes we got him awake. We asked him if he had a gun because we had seen a holster. This genius was so out of it he reached behind the passenger seat for the gun. He stopped when the three of us suddenly pointed weapons at him. After putting the vehicle in park, we got him out. As I was speaking to him, I could clearly see a plastic bag with a green leafy substance in it. The bag was on the floor between the driver's feet. As we removed the guy from the car, I pointed out the bag to the backup deputy. The driver was determined to be intoxicated. Under Alabama law because he was in an operational motor vehicle and was intoxicated, we could have put him in jail for DUI. But because I can cut people breaks, I figured we'd put him in jail for public drunkenness and for the marijuana (a misdemeanor from what I'd seen) and it would be a good first night for the trainee.

We hooked up the driver, and I told the trainee to start his pull-in form for the wrecker. After doing an inventory on the vehicle, we found twenty-six packaged bags of marijuana plus two sets of scales for weighing the product and more plastic bags for packaging. We ended up charging the driver with felonies.

After making the trip to the jail and doing the paperwork, we didn't leave until about four hours later than we'd expected. So much for letting the trainee off early. Still, it was a good first night out. When he came to work the second night, I asked him if he had gotten enough sleep, and he said he had. When we got in the car, I explained to him that not all nights would be like our first one. I recalled spending the night with one of my school chums when I was young. While we were watching late-night TV, his mother started screaming, "O Lordy Jesus." We jumped up and watched the house across the street burn to the ground. Not much fire protection in those days. The next day when my friend's dad took me home, he told me, "Rob, we appreciate you coming over, and you're welcome anytime, but just remember we can't guarantee a house will burn down every time." I told the trainee patrol was like that.

But it turned out I was mistaken. A house burned down almost every night while I had him in training. On our second night, we cruised around checking businesses and ran across what was probably about to be a robbery at a gas station. We pulled into the lot to do our check just a little before closing and saw two young males sitting low (as if they were trying to hide) in a car parked to the side of the station. We parked in front to check with the clerk about his knowledge of them, asking whether they were friends of his waiting for him to leave work. They pulled out quickly, turning into an apartment complex just behind the station. We got back in the car to catch up to them, and they turned in between two of the apartment buildings, trying to duck us.

It didn't work. We caught up to them as they were getting out of the car and walking toward the buildings. We stopped them to get IDs. One of them pointed toward an apartment building and said he lived there. When I asked him for an apartment number, he said he was actually visiting a friend who lived there. He didn't know the number and said they were looking for the Pebble Creek Apartments, a different complex about a city block from where we were. Okay, no big deal if you're from a different county. However, according to their IDs, they lived about a block from where we were. Still, they claimed they didn't know where Pebble Creek was even though there was an apartment complex located right on the highway with a big sign that said Pebble Creek Apartments.

I asked one of them if he had ever driven to Birmingham from his house. He said yes. When I asked how he usually went, he said Highway 78. I told him he drove right past the Pebble Creek Apartments every time he went to Birmingham. He stammered and didn't have an answer for that. We checked their IDs and sent them on their way. We followed them to the edge of the highway to see if they went to Pebble Creek. They drove right past the place even after the detailed directions we gave. We did a report and forwarded it to the detective division. We don't know if these two were ever matched to any of our robberies, but we know they didn't rob any business on our beat that night.

Later that night we were checking the roads for drunks and saw a car displaying a dealer drive-off tag. We figured we'd stop the driver to see what was up. Since I was driving this night, I went to the driver's side and the trainee backed me up. I told the driver the reason he was being stopped and got his license. I sensed something was odd because no one was sitting in the front passenger seat but there was someone in the back seat. I asked the driver if the vehicle was a new purchase and if he had the vehicle more than twenty days (the time Alabama gives you to buy a tag or transfer a vehicle to your name). He handed me the paperwork and admitted he'd had the vehicle for about two months.

While I was speaking with him, I could smell alcohol on his breath. I asked him about this, and he said he'd had a couple of drinks. Why is it always a couple? I asked him if it was a couple of cold beers or mixed drinks. He said he'd had some wine and mixed drinks. I asked him to step out of the vehicle and to approach the other deputy (my trainee). I asked the trainee to do field tests on him. I was going to obtain information on the passenger.

I went to the back door, and the passenger couldn't get the window down or didn't know how. I opened the back door when he unlocked it, and I asked him his name. He told me it was something like Jason Thomas. I got his birth date and asked for his Social Security number. He claimed not to know it (which is always a sign). I told him that wasn't a problem and asked if Jason was his first name. He said his first name was Michael. Why do most people use their middle name when they're trying to deceive? I asked him how he knew the driver, and he told me he had hitched a ride at a gas station and the driver was taking him to his parents' house just up the street. He tried to step out of the car, saying he had to pee badly. I told him to keep his seat and in a couple of minutes they would probably be on their way. I closed the door.

I returned to the driver just as the trainee was finishing up with him. I asked the trainee what he thought, and he said he thought the driver would be close on an alcohol reading. I asked if he wanted to put the driver on the portable breath meter and he said, "Why not?" I got it out of the car, explained it to the driver, and had him blow into the mouthpiece for a sample. Sure enough he was going to be close. As I was putting the meter back in the car, I heard the trainee yell, "He's running." I looked through the windshield and saw the driver standing where I'd left him. I looked past him and saw the driver's car speeding away. The passenger had jumped into the front seat and had driven away. This was the first time that had happened to me. I yelled, "Get in." We jumped in the car and took off. Unfortunately the car had a bad transmission and, as my daddy used to say, wouldn't pull a sick whore out of bed. After a short chase he managed to elude us but left the car where we would find it with the keys in it.

The trainee said he wished I could have seen my face when he yelled, "He's running," and I saw the driver still standing in front of the patrol car. I told him that I started to say, "He's standing right there," and that the look on my face couldn't have been as good as the look on the driver's face when we jumped in the patrol car and left him standing on the side of the dark road. He might well have been thinking, *Hey, he's stealing my car, and y'all are leaving me too.* I sent another unit to look for him and to bring him to us when we located his car. We kept him around for quite a while because we had to do some creative report writing and make sure he was well below the legal limit. Sergeant's orders.

The driver said he had stopped at a gas station and was giving the guy a ride. He said he didn't know the guy's name. We found out who he was, and it turned out he took off because he had warrants on him. After clearing it with the sergeant, I told the trainee that by now the driver was probably sober enough to drive home. It would be a long time before he would drink and drive again. After all, he had a nice jog in the dark running after us before the other unit found him. We cut him a break. That's about the only break we cut while the trainee was riding with me. We put almost everybody else we ran across in jail.

One night we were dispatched to a business where someone had broken into a woman's vehicle. I thought I'd help out the trainee by writing down the vehicle's tag number and the last six numbers of the VIN to make sure the tag wasn't switched. He was doing well with his training, and I didn't mind giving him a hand. After I got the tag number, I told him to get the woman's information and we could park up the street and complete the report. He got the basic report done, and I helped her knock some of the glass off the front seat because she was going to drive home. We went about a half-block away to finish up. The trainee got to the spot on the report where he needed the vehicle information, so I typed the tag into our laptop computer to get the VIN. Our laptops will give not only vehicle information but the registered owner's license information and report if the registered owner has any outstanding warrants.

When I put the tag number into the computer, bells went off. "She's got a warrant," the trainee said. "Are you sure?" I asked. He verified the information and said yes. We had taken someone to jail almost every night he was with me, but we hadn't this night. "Go back down there quick," I said. We eased back down the street. The woman was walking toward the business, carrying a broom she had borrowed to sweep the rest of the glass off her car seat. We pulled up to her, and after breaking the news, we took her to the jail. When we finished the paperwork on the arrest, it was almost time to go home, so we retreated to the substation to do the trainee paperwork.

The sergeant asked me if I felt it was fair to take the victim to jail. Couldn't we have arrested her later since we had good info on her? I explained that her warrant was for a felony (the fraudulent use of a credit card) and for a probation violation, which meant she hadn't paid her fine or hadn't shown up for court. Since she was going to jail and just had her purse with her checks and her credit card stolen, she might be getting a little bit of what she put someone else through. He seemed to understand a little better when I put it like that. I'm so charmed.

37

I Just Want a Sandwich

It never ceases to amaze me how much I cherish minding my own business or trying to help people out—or getting a sandwich. I could never meet the guys at a certain time or head off to get a sandwich without running across a DUI or an intoxicated person. Somebody had to go to jail. One time I was riding a two-man unit with one of my chums, and he said, "Let's go get something to eat." I said, "Sure," and looked up the highway to check for traffic before I pulled out. I saw a car parked near the side of the road with its headlights on. Being the thoughtful deputy I am, I pulled up to the car in the event the driver needed assistance. The car was running and in gear. The driver had his foot on the brake and was passed out. When we got him out, we discovered he was intoxicated. He went to jail. I just wanted a sandwich.

38

He Wasn't Drunk but Still Went to Jail

Another time I had pulled up to the parking lot of a local business to write a report when some excited citizens told me their motorcycle had been stolen and they knew where it was. They said it was in a mini storage unit just across the road from where we were parked. A local police department had captured one of the offenders, but two more were free birds. The captured one had confessed and had told police where the bike was hidden.

The citizens didn't know which detective was assigned to the case, but after I found out I gave him a call to have him tell me what I already knew. Nothing could be done in the middle of the night other than to take the information on the suspects, and he would get on the case first thing in the morning. I explained this to the citizens and then wrote up a report to be forwarded to the detective.

About two hours later, I saw two vehicles in the parking lot of the carwash located just beside the storage business. The citizens had given me the names of the other two suspects and vehicle descriptions. Neither of these vehicles matched the descriptions. Being the helpful deputy I am, I pulled over to check on the drivers in the event they needed assistance. They said they were putting some gizmos on one of the vehicles, and the carwash had good lighting, so they figured they'd do it there.

One of the vehicles had a personalized tag, which was kind of unusual, so I typed the tag information in the laptop. It turned out the vehicle was registered to one of the two other offenders in the motorcycle theft, and he showed an outstanding warrant. I asked them if the vehicle was one of theirs. One of them replied it was his. I told him he had an outstanding warrant and hooked him up. He wasn't drunk but still went to jail. And the detective knew where to find him when he wanted to talk with him.

39

Get a Room, Please

Blinders don't seem to work on me. People will park in the strangest places, and working the night shift you'll find them all over and in various states of undress. One night I was checking my businesses and visited a burger joint that had a twenty-four-hour drive-through. The place was always making suspicious person calls. It usually turned out that people had used the drive-through and had pulled into the parking lot to eat the food they had just bought.

One night the people at the burger joint called, and when I arrived I saw the vehicle they had reported. I pulled up behind it, gave the dispatcher the tag, and approached the vehicle. I saw a male asleep in the back seat, and in the front seat, big as life, was a woman breastfeeding her child. I don't know if they picked that up in the drive-through. I've seen a lot of things on this job, but very few embarrassed me like this did. I don't know why except maybe for the fact that the mama didn't seem to care. I called the dispatcher and told her that if she was going to send me to look at naked women she could at least have sent me to a supermodel.

Another time I was cruising around and decided to check under one of our river bridges where people will strip and dump stolen vehicles. I pulled up under it and sure enough there was a vehicle. I hit it with the big spotlight and saw a man and a woman straightening their clothes and buttoning their tops. I got both out and asked for identification. I then made sure both of them were there because they wanted to be and not because one had forced the other. After receiving their identification, I noticed they had the same last name. Fearing the answer, I asked, "Are you brother and sister?" They said no in unison. They explained they were divorced and had met up that night to try to get back together. Man, was I glad they said they weren't brother and sister. After all, we're not in Georgia. Get a room, please.

A local high school had a baseball field, and people liked to park behind it to do what they wanted to do. If you were back there and someone else arrived, you were to flash your headlights and they were to leave and find somewhere else or come back later. That way the people already there could have their privacy. I can't remember how many times I drove behind the baseball field and got headlights flashed at me. By this time I was close enough to hit people with the overheads or the big spotlight.

When they found out it was the police, they would always scramble to get dressed. Get a room, please.

One night when I pulled around, I saw a motorcycle parked back there, and when the lights got close a young couple jumped up half naked and ran behind the dugout. I grabbed the PA mic and told them to get dressed and to bring their identification to me. After checking the identification and making sure no one was forced to be there, I learned they were talking, just talking. I guess people can't hear each other when they have their clothes on. Maybe the clothing covers some secret voice box. Get a room, please.

40

Talking, Just Talking

One night I was riding with one of my chums, and as we were passing a small cemetery we thought we saw a car out there. Why are cemeteries such a draw to parkers? We thought we had some of those Satan worshippers or a coven of witches performing a virgin sacrifice or a carload of teenage drinkers. In any case there would be naked people involved. Hey, we were young and both guys. We pulled into the cemetery and found two cars—a large older-model sedan and a sheriff's unit. Hmm. We caught sight of a deputy, one of the old heads, a man who was so nasty I heard some female deputies say they would choose women if he were the last man on earth. A real prize, huh?

He approached us and said he and a friend were out there talking, just talking. They weren't doing anything, just talking. Nothing was going on out there. They were just talking. If he said they were just talking once, he said it fifteen times. I didn't know if he was trying to convince us or himself until I saw the woman he was talking to. I agreed with the female deputies: if he was the last man on earth and I was a woman, I would turn to women. And if he was the last man and she was the last woman, I would turn to myself. I'm not trying to bad-mouth anyone, but she was probably the female version of him. By the way, I wondered if he had been unable to hear her talking. Perhaps his gun belt had blocked his hearing and that's why he had taken it off. I usually wear mine around my waist, not my ears, and I've always heard fine.

We told him not to worry. We said we had come out there because we saw a vehicle and wanted to make sure no crimes were being committed. He said they were just talking. We drove away and said nothing for a while. I broke the silence by looking at my chum and saying they were just talking. I imagine our laughter could be heard for miles.

Oh, by the way, get a room.

41

Manatee-Size Ferrets

I was cruising around on the drunk patrol one night, and I noticed a vehicle parked on the shoulder of Highway 78. This was early in the shift and traffic was still heavy. A that time Highway 78 was the main route between Birmingham and Memphis. People were always breaking down. Most of the area on my beat was wooded, and it was dark in a lot of places. I knew I wouldn't want my wife or daughter breaking down in that spot, so I returned to check on the vehicle because I had seen it was occupied.

I pulled up with the overheads on and hit the vehicle with the big spotlight. I walked up to the driver's side, and when I shined my flashlight on them, the two people in the vehicle finally became aware of my presence. They were half naked and about to go at it like a couple of ferrets—manatee-size ferrets. I identified them after letting them get dressed. They explained they had several kids and never had any privacy. They had been to Birmingham for a business meeting, and this was about the only time they could have to themselves. But really! On the side of the highway? Get a room, please. I wondered if they realized that's why they had so many kids. Time to themselves.

About a week later I had a message in my mailbox at the substation to call this man. Having no idea what he wanted, I called him. After getting past the pleasantries, he hit me with the sales pitch. He wanted me to be an Amway sales representative. Thanks but no thanks. Overtime is just fine. Manatee-size ferrets.

42

Domestics

Domestic cases are sometimes interesting to work. Most of the calls involve husband against wife, but I've answered calls concerning son or daughter against mom or dad or against grandparents, boyfriend against girlfriend or one of their parents, in-laws against in-laws, and even girlfriend against girlfriend. I remember one case in which the victim didn't want to prosecute and the offender was gone when we arrived. We later found her intoxicated in a nearby ditch and took her to jail for public drunkenness. When we inventoried the vehicle for pull-in purposes, we found several sexual devices, which we listed as assorted hand tools. I don't recall answering any boyfriend-against-boyfriend calls. Both parties have usually made up before the court date, and it's true love again.

In one domestic case the mom and dad had assaulted each other. We had no choice but to take both to jail because of their actions and statements made. There were also four children at the house ranging in age from about two to eleven. We called the grandmother and asked her to pick them up and to care for them until the parents bonded out. When granny arrived we hooked up the parents and were leading them to the cars to be taken to the jail. We were in the middle of the yard when a half-empty soda bottle came flying between us, nearly hitting the backup deputy. We looked around and saw the culprit was a boy about nine years old, who was sitting on the top step of the family trailer. We were shocked. The handcuffed mom tried to make excuses for him. The other deputy said he needed to go into the house or he would go with us. The only reasonable excuse was that he hadn't had enough parenting. We'll probably be dealing with him by the time he's eighteen.

We had been to one address several times on domestic calls, but the offender (the husband) always ran off before we arrived. He was usually drunk and his wife never wanted him to go to jail, so she wouldn't sign warrants on him. One night he had beaten her up pretty badly, and I guess he wanted to get in a couple of extra hits. He didn't know my chum, who was going to the call, happened to be close by. The deputy arrived pretty quickly and this time saw which way the guy ran. He was caught, and on the way to the jail, he yelled from the back seat, "Go ahead. Take me to jail. I will get out and go back and kill that bitch. O. J. got away with it, and so will I." It was about one in the morning, so we called the judge and advised him of our past calls at the house and of the guy's record of not showing up for court. We also told him what the guy said about killing his wife and getting away with it. The judge put a $1,000 cash-only bond on the guy. That doesn't sound like a lot, but for this guy it might as well have been a $1 million bond because he wasn't getting out until a court date. It was a long time before we had to worry about him again.

There are also times when you feel a little bad about taking people to jail on domestic charges, mainly because one spouse will lie to have the other arrested. People know if they say anything about a crime being committed, our hands are tied and we must make an arrest. That's why I tell the new deputies I'm training to get a written statement from the victim. People will get to court and change their story, telling the judge they didn't tell the deputy what's in the report. In one domestic case, the wife (the offender) suspected her husband of having an affair and confronted him about it. The argument escalated and he said she threw a phone at him. He gave us a statement reporting this, and we hooked her up and took her to jail. Later I told the deputy who backed me up that I believed he just wanted momma out of the house to meet up with a sweet thing (just to talk, of course).

Sure enough when the case went to court, he told the judge he didn't tell us what he had said earlier. I produced a copy of the written statement, and when the judge asked him if that was his handwriting and his signature he said yes. The judge spoke to both parties and threw out the charge. The judge also wanted us to obtain a warrant on the husband for filing a false report, which we did. He told the husband he would find him guilty. The judge never took kindly to wasting deputies' time when we could be doing more important things.

43

Death

The law enforcement community often sees death. That's probably why it often doesn't get to us even when other people are deeply affected. I don't think we ever get used to death, but there is a sameness in dealing with it. We go to the scene, take a report, and then go to the next call. In Alabama if a person dies in someplace other than a medical facility or a nursing home, the sheriff's office is notified. We go to the site and act in place of the county coroner. We take a report and call the coroner, and if we find nothing suspicious, he gives okay for the body to be released to the funeral home. If there's anything suspicious or unusual about a death, evidence technicians and detectives are called and different steps are taken.

One death kind of got to me. It involved a kid, and kids always get to you unless you're a monster. This kid was a fourteen-year-old cancer patient who was spending the night with his grandparents. There was a do-not-resuscitate order involved. He had written a note (I don't know how recently) saying that he liked to spend the night with his grandparents and that he didn't want anything special done if he died. He shared other thoughts in the note as well. Most of the time when you answer a death call it involves an elderly person, but this time it didn't. I still see the model planes he had made or was working on. I thought about when I was young and building war models. I never thought about dying of cancer at his age.

Another death has always stuck out in my mind. I was patrolling the lower forty of my large territory when I received a call about a person who had shot himself. I was just about two miles away, so I arrived long before any backup. I saw a convertible Mustang parked in the front yard. Seated in the convertible was a male in his late teens. In his lap was a large Smith & Wesson revolver (a .44 Magnum) with his hand on it. He was still twitching, but for all practical purposes he was an organ donor. At this point I didn't know if he was alive or dead. As I approached, I unholstered my gun, not knowing what to expect. I grasped the revolver and took it from the male's hand. I put the gun in the trunk of the patrol car. Also at the house were an older female (the mother), who was hysterical, and an older male (the mother's boyfriend). There was also a younger female, the decedent's girlfriend, who didn't seem terribly bothered by the tragedy.

I later learned that a male teacher at a local high school had molested the teen boy. The teacher had been charged, and the case was coming up for trial. The mother believed her son was upset about this. I also learned that just before he went out and shot off the back of his head, he and his girlfriend had been arguing. I never found out about what. Could it be she told him he wasn't man enough because a man had done what he had done to him? The gun he used was his, according to his mother—a gift from her. Who gives a .44 Magnum to a boy in his late teens?

44

RV Road Rage

One night I got call about a road rage incident. A neighboring county sheriff's office was in pursuit of a brown RV pulling a white trailer. Someone in the RV was allegedly firing shots at another vehicle. According to dispatch, this was happening on one of the major interstates running through our state, and the vehicles were heading southbound into our county at speeds up to a hundred miles per hour. At the time I received the call I was less than one mile from this interstate and about ten miles south of where the vehicles were last reported. I figured I could drive to the interstate and sit for no more than a few seconds and the vehicles would soon be at my location.

I went up the interstate for about three miles but saw no sign of them. After waiting for several minutes, I spotted a two-tone motor home–type camper racing by at about eighty miles per hour. The camper was at least thirty-five feet long and pulling a sixteen-foot cargo trailer. This was a high-dollar camper. One of the other vehicles involved was ahead of the camper. I pulled out on the interstate and reached the vehicles but not before we got to a portion of the interstate that ran through one of our municipalities. The local police had three cars waiting for the camper. Word gets around. An evening shift unit was heading home nearby and came to back me up. We stopped the camper, and the other deputy got out with his shotgun. Two of the local police officers got out with their patrol rifles. There was no other county sheriff's unit.

I got on the rear corner on the passenger side, and after the camper's occupants understood we wanted them to shut off the engine (it was a diesel and therefore quite loud), we ordered them out one by one. The first one was a male in his late fifties who turned out to be the owner. I told him to grab the back of the camper. I found out how many others were in the camper and asked if there were any guns inside. He wanted to know what was going on and why he was being treated this way. I told him we would explain it to him shortly. All occupants were taken out and put into separate patrol cars until the whole mess could be sorted out. All the occupants said there was no gun in the camper.

The drivers of the other vehicles involved had been told to stop while they were on the phone with my dispatcher. After about an hour our county dispatcher and the dispatcher in the county north of ours had sorted things out and had determined in which county the incident happened. It took a unit from the other county another hour to get to our location.

I talked to the people in the two other vehicles about what happened and where. They said the incident began somewhere in Tennessee when the camper tried to run them off the road. They said they managed to get around the camper, but it sped up, trying to catch them. They said they had to do nearly a hundred miles per hour to escape the camper. They said the camper pulled off the interstate and they thought the incident was over. After they entered Alabama, they realized the camper had caught up to them and was trying to run them off the road again. They said they again tried to get past the camper, and as their lead car tried to pass, someone stuck a gun out the window and fired two shots in front of the car. As the second car went to pass, the gun appeared again and two more shots were fired. They again sped up in an attempt to get away.

I asked why they didn't slow down or stop and let the camper go ahead of them. Nobody likes my questions. The other deputy and one of the local police officers found a gun, a .38-caliber revolver. All of the camper's occupants denied the gun was theirs, and none of them had a permit to carry a handgun. The owner of the camper said the two cars had blocked him about twenty-five miles back. He said he was driving in the left lane, and one of them pulled in front of him and the other blocked him on the right so he couldn't get over to pass. He said they slowed him down to about sixty-eight miles per hour in a seventy-miles-per-hour zone. He said someone threw something out of one of the vehicles and hit his camper on the right front corner and someone again threw something out and hit his camper on the right side.

The neighboring county deputy arrived and took control of the case. The local police department charged the owner of the camper with having a gun without a permit and took him to jail.

45

Wrong Address

One problem we run into all the time is that houses are not marked with an address. People call and want help right away, but when we arrive in the neighborhood we can't find the house because it's not marked. This is certainly a problem for the night shift, often leading us to the wrong house.

One night one of my chums and I were working traffic on a highway when we got a call about a burglary in progress. The location was just off the highway and we were close by. We could catch the burglars. Another chum was on the other end of the road. Because we had units on both ends of a road, the burglars had to get past one of us. We had them hemmed in. We arrived, jumped out with guns drawn, and walked around the house, which was dark and appeared to be abandoned. There was nobody in sight.

Our other chum arrived and made contact with the person who had called to say his neighbor's house was being broken into. The deputy talking to the caller keyed up the mic and said, "Y'all at the wrong address." Maybe we couldn't catch the burglars. We found the right house and checked it. We discovered the incident resulted from an elderly person's eyes playing tricks. I don't know why, but this makes me giggle every time I think about it.

46

Burglary in Progress

One night we received a call about a burglary in progress. These
are usually bogus calls or false alarms, but this was a good one.
The owner of the house had rigged a monitor in his shed (he
called it a chicken house) and had the speaker in his house a
few hundred yards away. When he heard someone breaking
a window on the shed, he called the sheriff's office. We were
nearby and captured the guy. He had broken the window, but
the owner had so much equipment stacked in front of it there
was no way he could have gotten inside the shed. We took him
to jail and charged him with burglary. The district attorney who
screened the case barely managed to issue a burglary warrant.
He did so only because the offender had broken the plane and
was reaching inside or trying to take something.

I was shocked that the felony charge was issued because in a case
like this one our district attorney's office usually wouldn't want

to issue anything other than warrants for criminal mischief or trespassing (both misdemeanors). That's because the offender wasn't able to drag his whole body into the shed and to cart off a truckload of the victim's property. Sometimes I wonder how prosecutors sleep at night knowing how they're failing the people of the county. We often have enough to get a conviction, but we don't have enough to get a warrant.

47

Miscreants

On another night some young miscreants were driving around and busting open the change boxes on soda and "pay for air" machines. They had been down a long two-lane road and had hit several stores along the way. They were at a mom-and-pop store trying to break open the machines in front of the place.

Unknown to them, the storeowner had taken a page from the previous guy and had put a monitor out by his machines and a speaker in his bedroom. When they started sledgehammering his machines, he was awakened by the noise. He called the sheriff's office and went outside with his shotgun. He crept around the truck and surprised the young thieves, holding them until we got there. I believe they thought he would have shot them if they had tried to make a break for it. Even though they were going to jail, they seemed awfully glad to see us.

48

Criminal Division

When I worked in the criminal division I handled property crimes, thefts, burglaries, and forgeries. One day I was riding on a two-lane country road near our house with my wife and daughter when my wife said, "That looks like a motorcycle in the ditch back there." I turned around, and after another pass I spotted what she had seen. Someone had rolled a motorcycle into a ditch about nine feet deep. I located the VIN and called it in to the dispatch. The motorcycle turned out to be stolen.

I called a patrol deputy and he did a recovery. The motorcycle had been reported stolen about fifteen miles away, and it appeared whoever was riding the bike lost control and wrecked it at that point on the road. It also appeared to be going in the direction of the place where it was stolen. The bike was barely visible from the road, and if I didn't know better I would have been suspicious of my wife for having spotted it. I've always said everybody is a suspect except me and whoever is with me. She was with me.

49

An Insignificant Piece of Plastic

When I was a detective I worked a burglary case that still makes me grin when I think about it. Guns and electronics, including a large television, had been taken. We had no suspects, and no usable evidence had been obtained when the original report was taken.

I talked to the victim, and he asked me about a piece of plastic he had found in his driveway. He had told the original deputy about it. I said I did not know what he was talking about but would try to contact the deputy to see what he did with it. The victim told me he believed the piece of plastic probably broke off the burglar's car. I asked the deputy about the plastic and he had it. I told him I needed it because it might be evidence. I can still hear him saying as he gave it to me, "It's just an insignificant piece of plastic."

The small piece of red plastic was roughly triangular in shape. It looked like the inside of a car's door panel. The victim said his kid had a friend who used to come over. He said this was the only person he knew who had a red car. Because of some of the circumstances of the case, I had told the victim he probably knew whoever had done the burglary. A few days later a local police officer caught someone with the victim's shotgun and jailed him. I went to the jail and interviewed this guy about the shotgun. He told me who had given him the shotgun, and it was the person the victim had identified as having a red car.

I called this guy and he agreed to talk to me. He came in and I read him his rights and discussed the case. He denied having anything to do with the burglary or having any knowledge of it. He also said he did not sell the shotgun to the person caught with it. He was talkative, so I let the tape recorder run. After he finished I told him I had a few other questions. I asked him about his car, and he told me the make and the model. I asked if he had driven it to our meeting and if he would mind letting me take a look at it. He said I could, so we went outside.

I opened the passenger-side doors first and didn't see anything noteworthy. I opened the front door on the driver's side with the same result, but when I opened the back door it was a different story. There was a triangular hole where a piece of plastic had broken off from the armrest. When I put the piece I had in my possession in the hole, I looked at him and said, "Fits like it was made for this spot, don't it?" He hung his head and began to cry. He said he did the burglary and would tell me all about it. We went back inside and he gave me a written confession. When I went before the grand jury, the jurors got a kick out of the story about the insignificant piece of plastic.

While I was waiting for this guy to show up for the interview, a local bank investigator called me. My suspect in the burglary had cashed a stolen or forged check, and the investigator had managed to get a warrant on him. After I finished talking with the suspect, I called a patrol unit to take him to the jail on the forged check warrant. It just wasn't his day.

50

Slim Jim

One night toward the end of our shift we were kind of bored. We'd taken folks to jail, and it was early in the morning or late at night, however you want to look at it. A chum and I were sitting in our patrol car listening to the truckers talk on their CBs. There was a big truck stop nearby. We could hear truckers heading toward the truck stop ask truckers leaving if there was space to park. We could also hear the lot lizards (prostitutes) advertising their wares to the truckers. A guy was riding around with one of the prostitutes (probably his wife or girlfriend), and he kept saying, "Pills or Lucille? Who's looking for pills or Lucille?" He was advertising dope or sex, of course.

After a while my chum said, "Go ahead and talk to him." I keyed up and said, "How about that pills or Lucille?"

"Which one are you looking for?" the guy asked.

"Lucille, of course," I said.

He asked where I was, and I told him I had just pulled out of the truck stop and was heading west up the highway. He told me there was a parking lot to pull into, but I said I had just passed it. I told him this because I knew there were too many ways out of the lot and we couldn't hem him in there. He told me I would see a large chain store just about two miles up. We knew this store, and there was only one way in and one way out. I told him I would pull in there. He said he was coming that way. He asked me what my handle was. I looked at my chum because I didn't want to give this guy my real handle. I looked over at the passenger side of the patrol car and saw my car-opening tool lying there. "Slim Jim," I said.

"Okay, Slim Jim. What are you driving?"

"A big blue rig," I said. "Are you there?"

"Yeah," he replied.

My chum got up on a hill overlooking the lot, and I sat at a gas station across from it. As luck would have it, there was an eighteen-wheeler in the lot. And it was blue. This was just too good. We would swarm down on whoever showed up in the turning lane. The pill peddler and Lucille arrived and turned into the lot, heading toward the big rig. As it turned out, the driver of the big rig must have been listening because when the two started circling his truck and the pill peddler said, "I'm here, Slim Jim. Open the door," he began driving away. "Hey, where you going? Slim Jim?"

We followed the pill peddler and Lucille out onto the highway and stopped the vehicle. We let them know that we knew what they were doing and that we didn't want this in our jurisdiction. We didn't have enough to make a case that night, but we ran them out of our territory and told them to do their business elsewhere.

51

Accidents

It never ceases to amaze me how people gawk or rubberneck when they pass a traffic accident. It's as if they've never seen one before. They can't simply drive past an accident site. It doesn't have to be a bad accident, and it doesn't matter if there's no wreckage in the road. They just want to see the gore or stop and ask whether anybody got hurt.

One of the worst traffic accidents I ever saw was one I assisted on. I was riding with one of my chums. He was driving. We were on a dark two-lane road, and suddenly the kudzu started whipping up over my side of the hood. After the car found its way back onto the road, my chum pulled over and asked, "You want to drive, buddy?" We traded seats and I drove us around for a while before we decided to take a break at a highway intersection where a closed-down gas station was located. I was watching the traffic lights when a Jeep Cherokee ran through the light just after it turned red. I put the car in drive to make a stop but decided against it. No one had been at the intersecting road, and my chum was tired, so I figured I'd let him rest.

It's strange how things happen because of the actions you take or don't take. We had been at the intersection for a few minutes when the dispatcher put out a BOLO (be on the lookout) for a vehicle traveling the wrong way on the highway. The call was not ours, but because the driver was eastbound in the westbound lanes he was coming our way. We were about eight miles from where the vehicle was last seen. I put the car in gear and headed that way because if there was a traffic accident, it would more than likely be a bad one, and we'd be the closest unit to assist. We were heading up the highway when I looked over at my chum and said jokingly, "Who's got the airbag now, big boy?" We were in an early nineties Chevrolet that was equipped only with a driver's-side air bag.

The beat car was heading toward us from the other direction, and I thought that if the wrong-way driver didn't turn off, one of us was bound to run across him. The radio crackled, and the beat car deputy said he'd found the driver. He'd been involved in a traffic accident. It was a bad one too. The driver, who was intoxicated, was in a midseventies' Ford Ranchero, a big one. There was a tractor-trailer on the shoulder of the highway. The driver later told us he barely missed being in the accident. We originally thought he had been involved. The accident site was about a hundred yards off a big bridge. We arrived about thirty seconds after the beat car. A Jeep Cherokee sat mangled in the highway with some of its occupants hanging partly out of the wreckage. The Ranchero driver was pinned in his vehicle. The truck driver said the Jeep started around him and the Ranchero came across the bridge. He said he swerved to the shoulder and thought he was going to hit the bridge in avoiding the accident. One occupant of the Jeep had his head split open in front, with brain matter threatening to seep out. Both of a back-seat occupant's legs were jammed under the front seat and were broken backward. He had other injuries as did the rest of the Jeep's occupants.

I was assigned to ride with the driver of the Ranchero in the ambulance to make sure he didn't have anything to drink. The guy with the split head was being transported to the hospital in the same ambulance. Mr. Ranchero hollered all the way even though he had only a banged-up knee. Finally the paramedic told him to shut up. "You don't hear this guy carrying on like you, and his brains are hanging out," the paramedic said. "I don't care," Mr. Ranchero responded.

He was charged with vehicle homicide and went to court about two and a half years later. Mr. Ranchero had been in the jail the entire time. He had not made bond. He had time to sober up and to clean up. Four of us sitting in the courtroom had been on the scene that night. I think I was the only one who recognized him. He looked that different. It's not unusual for defendants to attempt to look like saints instead of dirtbags. They'll shave, get a haircut, and wear their Sunday best or a funeral suit. This guy had been in jail and hadn't had any help making himself look different than he did that night.

52

A Cat after Its Prey

One night I got a call to work a traffic accident that involved a vehicle rollover. The accident took place on a bad curve that a lot of people missed. They would usually shoot off the road, not roll. I thought this accident would probably involve different circumstances. I was right. Another deputy backed me up and I am glad he did.

When I arrived the driver had climbed out of the passenger side of a maroon Buick and was refusing treatment from the paramedics. He was about six four and 270 pounds. He was intoxicated. He had missed the curve and had rolled the Buick. Other than a small cut on his hand (which he let the paramedics wrap), he was uninjured. After getting information for the wreck report and the arrest report, I told the other deputy to get ready. I had told him about my plan. We were expecting the guy to buck us and were both surprised and glad he didn't. He could have been a handful because he was so big he had to sit sideways in the back of the car to fit. This was probably the only time I couldn't have fit another person if I had to be back there.

One evening I was working an extra shift and got a call about a vehicle rollover. When I reached the accident site, I saw a Jaguar in a cow pasture. The Jaguar had shot off the road, gone off an eight-foot bank, landed sixty to seventy feet off the road, and rolled over. I would have bet the driver was intoxicated, but he wasn't. He also had no injuries other than bumps and bruises. The Jaguar, which was totaled, did not belong to him. He said he had borrowed it from a friend. Ouch. He was trying to climb back into it when I got there. I told him it would probably be best if he waited until the wrecker turned the car back upright. He told me a deer had run out in front of him. I figured that cat, the Jaguar, had seen the deer and had chased after it, thinking it was prey.

53

Speed Kills, So Die High

One of the worst accidents I have ever seen was one in which my wife was involved. I didn't work this one but arrived after it took place. She had started a new job and had been there about two weeks. She was coming home when a white Ford Crown Victoria busted through a stop sign on a side road. She nailed it squarely in the right side just where the two doors meet. My wife had been having trouble learning the job and thought she wasn't going to make it. But this day had been a good one. She was coming home to wake me up for the night shift and to tell me she knew she would be able to do the job. She had decided we were going out to celebrate at a local restaurant; she loved the nachos and the chocolate cake at this place.

The Ford had three occupants, ages seventeen, eighteen, and nineteen. They were dirtbags, and I had made cases on two of the three. I have retraced their steps that day. I know that they had been to a local crack house, that they had bought beer, and that they had been run off from a funeral home parking lot for doing doughnuts while a service was taking place. I know all this from good investigative work. They had also been playing chicken (pulling out in front of cars to see if they would stop) at the intersection where the wreck occurred. They had just stolen gas and were making their getaway. They barely missed the truck ahead of my wife. That driver remembered a white blur.

When the two vehicles collided, the speed of the Ford threw both off the road. My wife's vehicle was pushed into a small bank nose first before turning over on its side and settling. The airbag deployed, saving my wife's life (Thank you, God), but the first impact crushed her ankle and broke her leg. It had to be rebuilt with pins, plate, screws, and artificial bone. When the vehicle rolled the airbag had already started to deflate. She was thrown forward and her head hit the doorpost at the jam. This caused a head injury that the hospitals didn't catch for nearly a week. She has never completely recovered from this injury. At the first impact when the airbag deployed it caught her arm and squeezed it against her chest. She was newly employed as a radio dispatcher, and the uniform she was issued had a silver badge. The impact left an imprint of this badge on her arm. She spent twenty-three days in hospitals, and at least five of those days were in the ICU.

Anyone who has lived with or known someone with a head injury, even a minor one, knows an injured person is not the same afterward. At this writing we have been married twenty years. When my wife had the accident we had been married ten. I feel like I have been married to two different women in the same body.

The occupants of the Ford got off lucky. They all died. In fact, when the deputies arrived they thought my wife was dead. The first two died on impact. They were seated on the passenger side. None of the three was wearing a seat belt. The driver was thrown out and landed partly under the vehicle. He was pronounced dead four hours later. The funeral home director who had run off the Ford from the funeral home property came over to view the accident scene and said it was the worst thing he had ever seen. He had to leave because he couldn't stomach it.

I was escorted by a deputy to the hospital emergency room where my wife had been taken. The ER crew had her in an area about twenty-five feet from the driver. I later heard that the deputy who escorted me to the hospital said he kept an eye on me because he thought I was going to pull the plug on this guy. I wouldn't have done anything to him there.

The hospitals did a lot for my wife. She was in two. She was taken to the first because it was the closest one with a trauma unit, but after she had been there six hours, the hospital said she would have to be moved. The hospital was not part of our insurance company's network. In other words, they had no agreement. I learned the next day that the two sides had been negotiating on an agreement for months. They reached one less than a month later. The doctor fought to keep my wife overnight to do more tests, and if he had been able to do that he may have found the head injury that wasn't discovered until nearly a week later. The doctor told me the insurance company said she was stable and had to be moved. The insurance company gave me two hospitals in the network to pick from and then had her taken by ambulance to the one I chose.

The company sent me letters and a representative called me telling me it initially paid for my wife's treatment only as a courtesy. The representative said the company's policy was that the person responsible for causing the accident was responsible for making good on medical bills the insurance company paid. Since that person was deceased, the responsibility fell on me, the policyholder. She said I signed the agreement. I told her this was not in any of the information the company had provided to me. I later learned no one else knew about this either. She said it was in the big book downtown—the complete policy information held at the courthouse. (It must have been in the finer fine print.) I told her I would take her word for it. She insisted that whoever was responsible would have to pay.

At this point I was mad and decided I had spoken with her long enough because she wasn't listening to anything I said. I told her if she wanted to collect from the responsible person, she could bring a shovel and I'd help her dig up the little son of a bitch and she could try to collect from his corpse. She never called me again, but she kept sending letters until I saw an attorney and had a letter sent that basically said the company couldn't collect a dime until it proved it had made my wife 100 percent whole. She tried to go back to work about six months after the accident, but because of the head injury she could no longer do the job.

My wife had to recuperate at home after she was released from the hospital. To break the boredom of being at home all the time, she would occasionally ride to town with me when I went to court. One day we were about ten minutes from the house, just going up the highway, when my wife pointed out a vehicle to me and said, "They're drunk." I saw a Ford Mustang, which had just passed us at a fairly high speed, running off the road. At this time we didn't have take-home cars, and we had just gotten walkie-talkie radios that we took home. We were in my pickup truck. I told her, "Just because they run off the road once doesn't mean they're drunk. Besides, it's only eight-thirty in the morning."

After passing us, the Mustang slowed down and we could see a white female at the wheel. She swayed across the highway lanes and then ran off the road again. At this point I told my wife I would stop the driver if I was in a patrol unit. We continued to follow her, and I told my wife that if the woman sped up I would not try to keep up. I got on the walkie-talkie to call in a report. We continued to follow the driver and gave the dispatcher updates on her location. She continued to sway across both lanes and to run off the road. At one point my wife said, "She's going to wreck." The Mustang ran completely off the road onto the grass median. The woman continued on the median for about a hundred yards and then pulled back onto the highway. For a moment it looked as if she would come up into the opposite lanes.

We followed her for about fifteen miles before somebody finally stopped her. I had to get the dispatcher to contact another agency to do this. I stopped in case this agency needed to put me down as a witness. The woman was high on pills. She had an all-day-size bottle of painkillers in her possession. The bottle had about 25–30 pills left in it, but the prescription had been written for 120 and had been filled just the day before. The other agency took her to jail, and we went on our way so I could get to court. My wife has gotten somewhat better, and I'm glad I still have her, but many problems remain from that day and have multiplied over the years.

54

Chicken Coop

When things were slow I would sometimes go to the interstate to work a little traffic. The best place to work it was just in front of the chicken coop. A chicken coop is what semitruck drivers call the little building at the weigh station alongside the interstate or the highway. At that time we could pull off in the middle and work both directions.

One night I had gotten a new strap for my uniform hat, and because things were slow, I thought this would be a good time to install it. I would turn on the radar unit, and any vehicles with radar detectors would get the signal and slow down. Instant traffic enforcement. To put the strap on, I had to loop it around a cord with two little buttons on the end. Some call them acorns but I call them nuts. I had the CB radio turned on and was listening to the truckers talk about me. A couple of them would joke about me sitting there with my doughnuts. I replied that I didn't have any doughnuts but that I was fixing my nuts.

I heard one of the truckers say, "He's needs to stop the car that just passed me at a hundred miles an hour." I keyed up to ask him where it was and got my answer. Just then a midnineties' Chrysler passed me. I clocked it at 104 miles per hour. I put down my nuts and pulled out to stop it. The Chrysler was southbound, traffic was heading uphill from the place where I was parked. I drove seventeen miles before I could catch up to the car and stop it. An older woman was driving the Chrysler. She was traveling alone. The Chrysler had Vermont tags, and she said she was on her way to Texas. When I asked why she was speeding, the woman said she was just trying to get there. With reasoning like that, I just had to try to write her a ticket. I did.

55

Stolen Gas

Another night I was sitting at the same spot in front of the chicken coop when one of the smaller police departments called to report a gas drive-off (theft) and gave a vehicle description and tag. I was about five miles away and thought, *I'm not close enough to try to help them out by looking for the vehicle.* No sooner had the thought left my brain when my luck kicked in. A vehicle matching the description passed my location. I pulled out and caught up with the vehicle, doubled-checking the tag with dispatch. The tag matched the information of the BOLO. I stopped the car, and the driver had no idea why. I had our dispatch notify the smaller police department. The officers came to my location and took control of the driver since gas theft was a misdemeanor. Charmed, I tell you.

56

Memorable Names or Events

Once while working as a detective I received a call in the middle of the night. A patrol deputy had captured a burglar in the act. When I arrived he had the guy in the back of his car. The burglar had glass fragments all over his clothes. The glass door at the front of the store was busted out. An evidence technician was called to process the scene. I opened the back door of the patrol unit and asked the guy if he wanted to talk. He said he would talk if he didn't go to jail. I told him I couldn't promise that because he was already headed there.

This guy had been a constant problem for the patrol guys. He stole property from neighbors and kinfolk, but nobody would prosecute or the courts wouldn't do anything to him because he was a juvenile. But he was eighteen now and old enough to go to the grown-up jail. I had the patrol deputy take him to the substation and sent another deputy to the county jail to pick up a set of jail clothes. We had him change into jail garb and sent his clothes to the forensics people to process. In processing the scene, the evidence tech took a section of glass from the door to compare it with the fragments on our suspect.

The guy denied breaking into the store, but he had a believable story. Sure he did. He said he had gone to his girlfriend's house and had just left when he heard the alarm going off. He said when he happened to pass the store the deputy arrested him. "No big deal," I told him. "Just give me your girlfriend's name and phone number so I can verify your story. We'll get this matter all cleared up and you can go."

"Well, I don't know her phone number," he said, "but I'll tell you where she lives."

"Okay, what's her name?"

"I don't know her name either. It's kind of a strange name."

"Not a common name?" I said.

"No. It's kind of hard to pronounce."

He was sent to jail that night on a burglary charge. The next day I went to the house where he said his girlfriend lived, and I made contact with a woman there. She was at least ten years older than my young burglar. But June-December relationships are not a big deal. She told me she knew him but he was not her boyfriend. She said he had been there for about four hours the night of the burglary. She told me he came by that night and she sent him away. She said after a short while he returned and knocked on her window to get her to the door. She said he tried to get her to let him inside, but she refused and he went away. She said while he was there, she heard an alarm going off. The house was located across the road from the store, separated by a small grove of trees. I asked her name and was expected something like Broom-Hilda or Drusilla, but she told me her name was Sandra. Pretty hard to pronounce, huh?

After the warrants are screened I pretty much forget about a case until I get a subpoena for court. Then I pull my case file. When I went to the grand jury on this case, the jurors thought the part about the so-called girlfriend's name was humorous.

It had been months since I had worked the case and I hadn't thought much about it. I was doing a lineup at a gas station on another case. It was after hours and close to the house, so my wife and young daughter rode with me. I had finished and had just got back into the car when I saw my burglar guy drive up. I knew he didn't have a valid license and would probably be good for an outstanding warrant. I had dispatch check the files, and sure enough I was right. I had dispatch start a beat car my way for transport, and I told the guy he needed to stay where he was because he had warrants. He didn't want to go and he started to fight with me. I grabbed him to handcuff him, but he slipped out of his shirt and took off down the middle of the road. I followed as best I could, but I was twice his age and fifty pounds overweight. A young, wiry patrol deputy arrived and ran him down. The deputy hadn't worked behind a desk for four years. The guy was hooked up and taken to jail.

I found out my young daughter was absorbing all of this. My wife said she had told her to get down low in the back seat. My wife said that when the excitement started she took her gun out from its hiding place. My daughter asked, "Mama, what are you doing?" My wife said, "Baby, I'm not going to let them hurt your daddy. If they try, I'm going to shoot them." My daughter talked about this incident regularly for more than a year and will still talk about it if you mention it to her.

57

I'm from Mississippi; No, Memphis

One night I was at one of my favorite spots—in front of the chicken coop—when I heard the truckers talking about a drunk. They always yelled about them because professional drivers had gotten used to us maintaining CBs in our units and knew we would get the drunks off the road. I keyed up to find out where this driver was and learned the vehicle was headed my way. I pulled out and got a description of the vehicle. I fell in behind it and followed it for a while to see how the driver was doing. I noticed the vehicle had a Mississippi tag. I stopped the vehicle after gathering probable cause. I determined that the driver was highly intoxicated. While talking with him, I learned he had just come from Mississippi. This guy had driven across almost a whole state. If I were to drink and drive, I would get stopped before I drove across the street. I'm not that charmed.

I was driving to work one night when the dispatcher reported that an off-duty deputy was behind a drunk driver. I picked up the pace to catch up to them. The vehicle was occupied by two people. Both the driver and the passenger turned out to be intoxicated. Both went to jail. The passenger insisted they had just three beers. At least I found someone who admitted to more than two! And he said they had just come from Memphis. They didn't know where they were either. When we did the pull-in for the vehicle to be towed, we discovered he probably was telling the truth. They probably did have just three beers. The cold beer they had left was quart size. Memphis is about a five-hour drive from Birmingham, and it would take me a drive from Memphis to Birmingham to drink three quarts of beer.

58

Next Time I'm Calling in Sick

I've often accused my wife of being clairvoyant. One night I was working an extra shift on my off night, and she begged me not to go in because she felt like something bad was going to happen. She said she didn't feel like it would happen to me but to someone close. I told her the shift was short and I had to go in because I had signed on to work. I told her I would be careful. I didn't think much else about it. I rode around for a while trying not to do too much because I was on the clock. This was like free money, and all I had to do was show up for it.

I pulled into a redneck bar and saw two guys standing in the back of the lot next to a vehicle. Judging by the surprised looks on their faces when I pulled up, they had probably just urinated in the lot or had just finished a dope deal. I had a weird feeling about them, like when the hair stands up on the back of your neck, but I got out to talk to them anyway. As I was getting out of the unit, the dispatcher put out a call saying an officer was down. My wife's premonition came back to me. I told the two guys that the bar they had just left had a working restroom. I didn't do much else because the dispatcher updated the information to say a deputy had been shot.

At the time we had seven substations, two jails, and a headquarters building. Our radio system operates on three channels. On the channel I was monitoring the radio had been quiet. Nobody was out on a call. I learned an off-duty deputy had been working a part-time job and was ambushed. He died instantly from the wounds he received. I had known this deputy since before I started with the sheriff's office. That's fairly close. He worked in the same office as my wife when she was a civilian clerk with the sheriff's office. I was pulled closer into town but never made it to the scene. My chum did. That morning before we were off duty we were gassing up the cars. I told my chum about the feeling my wife had the night before and how she asked me not to go to work. This was the first time I had told anyone. He told me if she had that feeling again I should call him and he would call in sick.

59

Unsuccessful Officer of the Year

For a while when I was working as a detective, I was allowed to come out on the weekends when patrol was short to work extra shifts. Free money. On one extra shift I was dispatched to take a report on a stolen motorcycle. When I arrived dispatch advised me not to pull into the driveway because evidence might be located there. I took the report and talked to the neighbors to find out if they had seen or heard anything. I did this because I knew I would be getting the case Monday morning when I returned to work. The neighbors had some leads, and I wasn't too busy (no pressing calls), so I was glad to follow up with them. They had the VIN (which most people don't), and they even gave me photographs to use for comparison.

The possible evidence they had was a shoe print, and they wanted a cast made. I called the sheriff's evidence technician about the cast, and he said a shoe print was like a tire print. They're all alike when they roll off the line. I knew already this. He said what any flaws, scars, or other defects can be used for match. I knew this too. The bottom line was that it was Sunday, and he didn't want to come out to do an impression since we had no suspect shoe to compare it against. This I could have guessed before I called. The victim ended up making a cast of the footprint and getting it to the evidence technician the next day.

The leads the victim had didn't pan out. The neighbors called with more, but the motorcycle was never recovered. At one point the victim told me she was willing to go undercover in the biker world to help find the motorcycle. She told me she had worked for a police agency. She said she still had wigs and trashy clothes if she was needed. I passed her offer on to my supervisor just as a courtesy. It didn't happen. I knew it wouldn't. Though the motorcycle was never recovered, the victim wrote a letter to the sheriff telling him what a great job I did handling the case. It went in my official file. I worked with two other detectives at the time. They were Abbott and Costello types. They put together an award for me for the outstanding job I did—Unsuccessful Officer of the Year or something like that. They thought it was hilarious that somebody could get a letter for not solving a case. It's the only award I've ever received.

60

We've Got Enough for a Conviction—We Just Don't Have Enough for a Warrant

Like everything else, working as a detective had pluses and minuses. One big minus was dealing with our county district attorney's office. The people there would spend more time trying not to issue a warrant in a case than it would take to issue a warrant, jail the person, and go to a preliminary hearing.

I found one case particularly annoying. A man thought his stepson had broken into his house and had stolen an air compressor and a pressure washer. The stepson had stolen from him in the past, but the victim's wife had always talked him out of putting the stepson in jail. The wife had passed away a few months earlier, so this time when the stepson broke in and took stuff there was no one to talk the victim out of putting him in jail. A neighbor had seen the stepson at the victim's house on the day of the burglary and had picked him out of a lineup. The victim said the stepson had admitted to taking the items and had told him where he took them.

I tried to make contact with the stepson, but he wouldn't come in to give his side of the story. I took this information to the district attorney's office and had to beg for a warrant. I still don't know how much more proof these people wanted. The assistant DA I screened with typed a brief synopsis similar to what I described above. At the end she typed these two lines: "Unfortunately, we have nothing other than the victim's word that the defendant confessed. Since we have probable cause we have no choice but to issue."

Unfortunately we have nothing other than the victim's word? How about the fact that a witness put the stepson at the house and picked him from a photo lineup or that the property was found where the victim was told it was? I was a little more than pissed. But after we screen with the assistant DAs, we walk back up to the front, and a secretary types up the results. I saw the last two lines and had to have a copy for my file. I don't know if I was supposed to get one, but I managed to charm a copy from her. Probable cause? What do they think they're supposed to operate on, positive cause? I thought that was for the court to decide.

61

That's How It's Supposed to Be Done!

I've never believed in selective law enforcement. I don't care if you're a prince or a pauper, a stranger or a brother. If you're doing wrong you should go to jail. My wife and I have kinfolk who don't operate entirely within the limits of the law 100 percent of the time. Some of these people I know by name, some by sight, and some by their nicknames.

One night I was dispatched to a small police department just outside of our county to pick up a prisoner the local agency had arrested on our warrants. That the prisoner pickup should be at the police department was kind of strange because usually when an agency runs across someone with outstanding warrants officers will stand by on the side of the road until the other agency gets there. The dispatcher had given me the name, and it was something like Don Phillips, which didn't mean anything to me. When I got to the jail the officers were standing in their dispatch office. A wall with another door separated that area from the jail. The officers looked as if they had been in a fight.

"They just sent one of y'all," one of them told me as I walked in the office.

"How many do you need?" I asked.

"He's a fighter," the officer said. "He might be a problem."

I broke the snap on the case on my belt that held the pepper spray canister, pulled it out, and shook it a few times. "I've got something that'll probably take the fight out of him," I said. "Go ahead and open the door."

We went inside the jail and I saw my wife's cousin. I knew him only by his nickname, but since this was the South, it could just as well have been his given name. I'll call him Bo. He was standing in the jail cell, gripping the bars like a trapped wild animal. When he saw me his whole demeanor changed. "I've got him, fellows," I said. "Just give me a couple of minutes. I'll be right out." The officers went back outside and I asked him, "Bo, what did you do?"

"I don't know," he said. "I was just sitting in the parking lot, and they came up and said I had to go to jail. But I hadn't done anything."

It turned out Bo had gotten into a row with his girlfriend, a common occurrence for him. This time she had signed a warrant on him. Well, Bo didn't know, and Bo was what some would call slow. All Bo knew at the time was that he was sitting in the parking lot minding his own business when the police showed up and said, "You're going to jail." The police may or may not have known how slow Bo was and may or may not have explained things in a way he could understand. Anyway, Bo got taken to jail fighting all the way.

I told him he had to go to my jail. I had him turn around and I hooked him up. I led him out of the jail and to my car. When we passed the officers, he looked at them and said, "You see. That's how it's supposed to be done." I don't know what they thought I did, but because of what he said they thought I was some kind of superman. We went to the jail without incident. And I never told those officers Bo was my wife's cousin. That was my little secret.

62

Repeat Customer

A few years later I saw Bo driving around and knew he had recently been to jail. My in-laws always told me whenever he had made visits because he always called my paw-in-law to talk. I think he was the only person who would accept the collect call from the jail. And I knew Bo had a habit of not showing up for court. I had dispatch check the files, and sure enough he had outstanding warrants. I was working the detective division and didn't have a screen in my car. I was also in the habit of going without handcuffs.

I radioed a patrol unit and turned around to see if I could locate Bo. I found his vehicle at a nearby gas station, waited until he came out, and carried on a conversation with him until the patrol unit arrived. When the patrol deputy got out, Bo became anxious, thinking something was up. We told him he was under arrest, and he acted as if he was going to drive away. The patrol deputy unholstered his gun and told him he was going to shoot the tires. Bo jumped out of his truck and raced behind the gas station.

Bo was less than half my age, and the patrol deputy was even older than I. He was also built like a gazelle and ran like one. We looked for him for about two hours, and other deputies showed up to assist. He got away that day but was later picked up on the warrants. He later told me he had climbed a tree and was hiding in the vines, watching us look for him. I guess a gazelle was the wrong animal to compare him with.

On another occasion a night-shift car was sent to pick him up from another agency. On the way to jail he started squirming in the back seat. When the deputy slowed the car to see what he was doing, Bo kicked out the window on a rear door and crawled out if it, running off into the darkness. He got away that night but was later picked up, and the judge set a no bond on him. I guess the judge was trying to break Bo of his bad habit of not showing up for court.

63

Bad Shot

One night we received a call about a fight at a redneck bar. We didn't get many calls from this place, but when we did the situation was usually pretty bad. When we got there we saw that four people were separated from the rest of the customers. After a little investigation we learned these four were the troublemakers. Big surprise. One the four was a female who had assaulted another female in the bar. One of the three males was older than the rest and was the group's leader. When the call went out four of our units were dispatched. Our sergeant also showed up. This bar was known to have been a rough place in its day, but the patrons were mostly up in age, so they had mellowed. They probably felt like they had already done their share of fighting.

When we went to arrest the female, the three males said we weren't gonna take her. Wrong. We ended up taking all four of them to jail. I hooked up three and needed one more pair of cuffs. I borrowed another set, and another deputy hooked up the last prisoner. We led them outside to the cars, and I was going to load up the four in the car I was driving. The sergeant told me to divide them up and let somebody else take two. I told him I would do whatever he wanted, but I believed if they were arrested together they should ride to jail together. My plan was probably the better idea. We had about a thirty-mile journey to the jail, and that was the main reason the sergeant wanted the four divided up.

We took off for the jail. I had the female and the leader male. I was in the lead vehicle. My backup deputy took the two followers. We had to travel a long, dark two-lane road that turned into a four-lane highway closer to town. We were about eight miles into our ride when the deputy said, "Pull over up here." I pulled over at little business along the highway. I got out of the car as the other car entered the parking lot. It hadn't come to a complete stop before the deputy came bouncing out. "That son of a bitch shot at me," he said. This deputy was usually super calm and rarely used profanity, and until this point I had never seen him angry. We aimed our weapons at the guy in the back seat whom the backup deputy pointed out. He dropped his gun and the deputy retrieved it.

Somebody had missed a gun on this guy. In the process of getting the four hooked up and loaded into the cars, he was passed around and possibly didn't get patted down. At least that was the story. I searched my two even after they had been given to me and supposedly searched. If I must do some Monday morning quarterbacking, I would say a deputy missed the gun. He was the one who compared handwriting samples to figure out who wrote the fake escape letter we planted in the jail. Anyway, the guy had the gun hidden on him, and while he was in the back seat, he managed to reach around his skinny body, pull it out, and fire it toward the deputy. Luckily he couldn't get a straight-on shot. The bullet hit the top protective screen. It was a glancing strike and the bullet fragmented. Part of it went over the protective screen and struck the deputy in the back of the neck. "Didn't know I had a gun, did you, motherf——?" the guy told the deputy.

I was mad, but when the sergeant showed up, I learned what mad looked like. After the trip to the jail, we ended up writing reports the rest of the night. We learned a lot that night. For me, the main lesson was that no matter how many times prisoners have been searched, one more search can't hurt. And I still say if the sergeant had listened to me, this may not have happened. The four would have been packed so tightly, the prisoner couldn't have gotten that gun. If they're arrested together they ride together.

The shooter went to court and drew a prison sentence. A few years after he got out, I was working as a supervisor and units were dispatched to a traffic accident with a fatality. Supervisors also respond on these calls. On a two-lane country road a driver crossed over the line and struck our shooter's vehicle head-on, killing him instantly. This time he was just minding his own business, coming home from the grocery store.

64

Go Home or Go to Jail

I've always had a reputation for knowing how to bust up a party. More than once I've walked into a redneck bar and told the people causing trouble, "Go home or go to jail." It was their choice, and to show them I was a man of my word I've taken people to jail. You don't have to do this too many times before people will leave the minute you walk inside. This cuts down on problems such as fights. When people are intoxicated, they will usually get loud and brave. This rubs someone the wrong way and words are passed. Then fists fly. If you are assigned to keep the peace, you will do it any way you can.

Another phrase I'm famous for is "Turn on the lights, and turn off the music." Redneck bars often have loud music and the lights are fairly dim. It's hard to talk to a crowd under those conditions and get your point across. One night I was driving through the parking lot at a late-night go-go bar and saw a young-looking kid stumble out and get into a Ford van. I pulled up to him to check on his welfare. I determined he was intoxicated, hooked him up, and took him to jail. I also found out he was only nineteen. You have to be twenty-one to legally consume adult beverages. You must also have proper identification to get into one of these establishments. He had identification and that's how I knew how young he was.

A week later I was driving through the parking lot at the same bar. Parked in the lot was the same Ford van. Had this kid learned nothing? I parked and went inside. There were fifteen to twenty people in the bar including employees. Standing at the bar with his back toward me was the same kid. He turned around with a pitcher of beer in each hand. When he saw me he looked rather surprised that I had caught him. He set down the beer and I told the bartender he was only nineteen. I also told the bartender to turn off the music and turn on the lights. I then went around the room and collected identification from everyone who had it. Under the law you're not allowed to enter a bar without identification. I told those without it to sit at a corner table.

I radioed the dispatcher and said I needed warrant checks on fifteen identifications. The next voice I heard over the radio was the sergeant telling the dispatcher to send more units to my location. I thought, *I'm here and I've already got this.* The sergeant and two patrol units arrived as I was running the persons with no identification out of the bar. They couldn't stay because that was against Alcohol Beverage Control Board rules. Only one person in the bar went to jail that night. After that night I made it a regular routine to go by this bar. Turn off the music and turn on the lights.

65

Daddy's Girl

When you work this job for any length of time, it's common to get your share of bumps and bruises. I've been off work numerous times with injuries, once for a few days and once for six months. One doctor even said I had fractured one of the vertebrae in my back. One quack I saw said this injury was in my head and called the sheriff's office administrators to tell them so. I've also had what they call a boxer's fracture in my hand.

One night I was going into work and heard a call go out about a domestic situation in progress. The deputy responding had to go solo because there was no other unit available. I volunteered to go on the call with him. When we arrived we discovered that the mama had been knocked around and held against her will and that the daddy was intoxicated and was threatening to burn the furniture after piling it up in the front yard. He had already started a fire and was cursing and threatening us. When we attempted to hook him up, he began to fight us. During the fight I swung at him. He either dodged the full blow or I just missed, but I made contact with his skull, fracturing my hand.

Never again will I hit anyone with my hand. I now adhere to the children's rhyme about sticks and stones, and that is what I use. I had dealt with this individual before when he was intoxicated, and he was never like this. I was a bit baffled. His sister showed up while he was in the back of the car about to go to jail. She said it was not how much he drank but what he drank that made him like that.

The upside of most of my injuries was that my daughter was young and I got to spend a lot of time with her. During these times, when she was near and observed me, I was able to make a real daddy's girl out of her.

66

He'll Never Look at Santa the Same Way

We sometimes work in secluded parts of the county. At night most businesses are closed, and restrooms aren't always available in these areas. Many of the local fire departments give us access to their stations via a key or a combination to their locks. The fire station usually offers a flat spot to do a traffic accident diagram, and it's a good place to be when nature calls.

One night during the Christmas season nature made this call, and I headed for a fire station. While I was doing my business, one of my chums came by the fire station to meet up with me. He was waiting outside in the station's common area when the sergeant called, saying he wanted to meet with him. My chum told him he was at the fire station, and the sergeant said he would be right there. The firefighters had recently been in a Christmas parade, and Santa had ridden on the fire truck. He had left his red suit at the station. My chum had small kids and thought it would be a neat idea to dress up in the fire station's Santa outfit and take a photo to show his kids. He yelled at me to hurry up and get my Polaroid camera to take his picture. I had no idea he was dressing up.

I was just leaving the restroom and was hooking up my gun belt as the sergeant came through the front door. I'll never forget the look on his face when he saw me putting on my gun belt as my chum stood nearby in a Santa Claus suit. All he said was "I don't want to know." When the story got around, I don't think the other deputies on the shift or the majority of the sheriff's office employees looked at my chum and me the same way again.

67

She Fished Out the Jet Ski

I was working an extra day on the day shift to earn some free money when we were short on deputies. I got a call about a missing person down at the river. A guy had taken his Jet Ski there late at night and had not come home. His wife and his brother went to the river the next morning not to look for him but to fish out the Jet Ski to take it home. The guy's mother had called when she found out he never made it home.

The call came in early in the shift, and I spent all day on it, getting home just before dark. At that point the search was called off until the next day. It was summer, and even though I wore my hat I received a sunburn so bad my head was as red as a dashboard warning light.

Two rescue squads responded and stayed out on the river, looking all day and into the night. A helicopter searched a wooded area in case the man had left the river and had gotten lost in the woods. His body was found in the river the next day. He had drowned. He was about twenty feet from where the Jet Ski was fished out. I still wonder why his wife fished out the Jet Ski but didn't report him missing. Worst sunburn I have ever had. Bet my head peeled off three times.

68

Big-Truck Protocol

There's a reason we have guns. On several occasions I probably wouldn't have survived if I hadn't had a gun and the other person did or if that person hadn't had my gun pointed at him and didn't think I would use it. I have had to display my gun more than once to deter harm to myself or to others. I have even walked up to a driver's door with a gun at my side on a car stop because something didn't feel right. We work one-man units, and my usual beat was about twenty square miles, pretty large for our county. And it was one of the remoter beats. That meant backup was several minutes away. The wait can seem a lot longer when you're fighting somebody or holding a suspect at gunpoint.

One night I stopped a car for a bad tag. The driver pulled over, and as I prepared to exit my vehicle three Hispanic males bailed out and ran toward me. I pointed my weapon at them and shouted at them to stop. They did. I yelled for them to get back in the car. They did. I approached the driver and asked for his license. Suddenly none of the three could understand English. I don't speak Spanish, so we had a problem. The car had a bad tag and the driver couldn't produce a license. I couldn't understand them well enough to write a ticket. I wasn't going to let them drive without seeing a license, so I told them, "You no drivey drivey. You walkey walkey. Now vamoose." The last I saw of them they were walking the final quarter-mile to where I think they said they lived.

On another night I stopped a pickup for a traffic violation. As I got out to approach the vehicle, the driver exited the truck and walked around the front, away from traffic, and came toward me on the passenger side. I later learned this was a big-truck driver. I had not seen this before and didn't feel good about it, so I unholstered my gun, and by the time he reached me, he was staring down the business end of my weapon. He stopped. I was new to the patrol division and didn't know highway patrol officers and state troopers like truckers to exit their big trucks and walk back to the patrol units. I deal with drivers of private vehicles on 99.9 percent of my stops. The other 0.1 percent are big-truck drivers. I know now how to tell if the driver is a big-truck driver.

69

Fear Levels

I was working another free-money shift when the day shift was shorthanded. I stopped a vehicle for speeding, and the driver turned out to be suspended. While I was writing his tickets, I wasn't aware that he had gone back inside his vehicle to retrieve something. As I left my car with the ticket book in hand, he suddenly reached back inside his vehicle and grabbed something that was hidden from my sight. By the time he stood up I was pointing my weapon at him, yelling for him to show me his hands. When he did, I saw he was holding some folded papers. Afterward I was glad it was daylight because in the darkness with just a spotlight on him I would probably have shot him for making a move like that. My fear level rose that quickly.

One night I stopped a man for speeding. I decided to give him a written warning and told him so. I explained this wouldn't go on his record and he wouldn't have to go to court. I went back to the patrol unit to write the warning and returned to his vehicle for him to sign it. As I started to walk away he thanked me and said he wanted to give me something. He reached inside the truck and I thought he was going for a gun. My fear level rose again. I started unholstering my gun, but when he turned to face me he had a small plastic bottle in his hand. He said, "This is the best gun-cleaning solution you can get." He had some connection with the folks who made it. He told me that it wasn't just a lubricant and that it would get a gun cleaner than any other product. He said his son was an officer in Tennessee and during a struggle had gotten blood on his Sig. He said his son cleaned the gun with this product and it took the blood off.

I thanked him but told him he didn't have to give me anything. He said he wanted to because he knew police weren't appreciated enough. There was a toll-free phone number on the bottle, and still thinking I might have been given a product that would dissolve my weapon, I called it. A young lady answered and in a cheerful voice said, "Kill-a-cop hotline." Just kidding. When I told her the *Reader's Digest* version of the story, she said, "You must have stopped Mr. Smith. He's always giving away bottles of the product. He's very proud of it." I've used the cleaner since that time and it does a great job.

197

70

Light versus Knife

I was working the evening shift and got a call about a burglary in progress. As usual the call came in from a neighbor. I was close and got there quickly. I went around the house where the offender was last seen. He was just inside the den and had a knife in his hand. The homeowner was also there, and as it turned out the offender was his son. I had unholstered my gun as I got out of the patrol unit. I pointed my weapon at him and flipped the switch on the laser sight I had recently installed. The red light came on and I centered it in his chest. I told him to drop the knife but he refused. The homeowner told me not to hurt his son. I said, "Mister, I'm about to kill your son unless he drops that knife."

The two were often involved in domestic situations. When I arrived, the son was threatening his dad with the knife. I think I convinced him it was in his best interest to drop the knife, because he did so. When the backup arrived, we hooked him up and took him to the substation to talk to a detective. For a change his dad wanted to prosecute in this case. The son had done this before, and the family had never done anything in response. I guess these people had had enough or didn't want the red light to return.

71

It's Hot, Real Hot

One night I stopped a pickup for reckless driving. This was shortly after we had been certified to carry pepper spray and had just been issued it. We got certified by being sprayed with the stuff. It burns real bad. I had thought there would be a written test instead. After talking with the driver and doing field tests on him, I determined he was intoxicated. He had gotten mouthy, asking me why I had stopped him when he wasn't doing anything wrong. I told him he was under arrest for DUI and ordered him to put his hands behind his back. He wheeled around and hit me in the chest, saying, "You're not taking me to f—— jail."

I was wearing my bullet-resistant vest, so the blow did not injure me, but I was angry because of the sucker punch. I unsnapped the holder that housed the can of pepper spray, pulled out the can, and, as recommended in the certification class, gave him one to two seconds of spray. This was the first time I had used it, and boy was I impressed. His eyes slammed shut and he started screaming, "Why did you do that?" He no longer had any fight in him, and I hooked him up with no further problem. His eyes never opened before we got to the jail, and he had a snotsickle down to his knees. He refused the alcohol test when I got him to jail, but when I called the jail to find out when he got out, I was told when deputies finally did a test on him about twelve hours after I had dropped him off, he was still over the legal limit. Man, was he drunk.

I learned pepper spray would work under just about any condition. It was probably better than sticks and stones. After we had pepper spray for a while and had a chance to use it on something besides vicious dogs, we came up with cute nicknames for it—the can of death, resist no more, and my favorite, karate in a can. It's hot, real hot.

72

Everybody Has Quirks

While I was a field training officer, I worked with all kinds of people. These people had worked with other FTOs, and some had quirks. Everybody has quirks, but these trainers had some unusual ones. I saw FTOs who wouldn't let rookies drive their assigned units and yet gave them grades on driving. Some wanted trainees to walk backward when returning to the patrol unit during traffic stops. What's wrong with glancing back over your shoulder? They wanted trainees to keep a hand on the ticket book while having the driver sign the ticket. Did they think the driver would steal that $3.50 form holder? I've always let drivers hold the book to sign. So they keep it and drive off? The sheriff is out a few bucks, and I get to charge them with theft and put them in jail. I know who they are.

Some FTOs wouldn't go anywhere to eat when they had a trainee. I know of trainees who survived on popcorn and coffee during the four weeks they were with training deputies. They ate whatever they could grab while gassing up the patrol car. Some FTOs made trainees eat a certain meal at a local truck stop and said they wouldn't pass them to the next phase if they didn't. One meal consisted of a country-fried steak that looked like a hubcap from a 1973 Ford and was probably about as tasty. I always told rookies they could take a little from each training deputy and could add what they knew to develop their own style.

When I was off, the other training deputy on the shift would take my rookie, as I would his. One of his rookies had to ride with me in the last week of her training. On the first night I handed her the key and told her it was all hers. I would sit in the passenger seat and observe, and if she had any questions I was there. She had been graded on driving even though one training deputy never allowed her to drive and another let her drive for only a week. One night while we were riding the area we got a call to the interstate. We were told a tanker containing eighty thousand gallons of gasoline was on fire. After grabbing all the cans we could carry, we were off. After all, gas was $3.50 a gallon. Joke.

We were on the southbound side and the tanker was on the northbound side. Local police had already arrived along with the fire department, and those guys were right on the tanker, putting water to the fire. They were a lot closer than I would even think about getting. I told the trainee to drive to the next exit and to come back up on the other side. The highway patrol had sent troopers, and they were on the way to work the scene. That made things easier for us. A local police officer was stationed beyond the entrance ramp, trying to hold traffic, so I told the trainee that when she got to the top of the ramp, she should drive down there to see if he needed assistance.

"You mean drive down the wrong way on the interstate?" she asked.

"South in the northbound lanes," I told her. "We can do that."

"Cool," she said.

She drove like she was doing it for the first time and enjoying it. The traffic was stopped and another local police officer arrived to help his buddy, so we returned to where the firemen were squirting water on the eighty thousand gallons of gasoline. They got the fire out, and I told the trainee to go back down to the other end and we would open up traffic. She returned with the same excitement she had the first time. She got a call from one of her buddies at the jail. The people there usually monitored patrol radio traffic. While she was talking with her friend, I heard her say, "I got to drive the wrong way on the interstate."

"Twice," I said.

"Twice," she told her buddy. You would have thought she had won the door prize at an FOP meeting. Sometimes it's the little things that make me appreciate this job.

73

Traffic Enforcement

I had another trainee whom I thought was going to be idle but who turned out to be a hard worker. He wrote a good report when he came to me but had not made a single traffic stop during the first phase of training. I remedied that soon after he came to me. I installed a radar unit from the station in the patrol car, and away we went. After a few days of clocking cars and writing tickets and warnings, he couldn't believe how many people we were stopping. He was also amazed at how often we flashed the blue lights at people to slow down. I told him several times he could fill up a ticket book (twenty-five forms) and a warning book (fifty forms) every month without trying. After a few days he believed me.

One night we were listening to the truck traffic on the CB. The trainee commented that the truckers had their own language. About this time the truckers mentioned a drunk driver on the highway. I keyed up and started talking to them to get a location. After locating the vehicle and following it, we stopped the driver for probable cause and found him to be intoxicated. He went to jail. I later told the trainee that until I got to the driver's window and spoke to him, I thought he was an old woman. I didn't realize the driver was a man until he turned and spoke to me.

Another time we had just left the jail after taking in an intoxicated person. We got on the interstate and weren't a quarter-mile from the jail when I told the trainee to watch a particular car. The vehicle was in the middle lane, and the driver strayed back and forth over the lines on either side. He pulled over to one side until he was in front of us and sped up. He shot across both lanes and almost hit the concrete barrier separating the northbound and southbound lanes. He slowed down, turned on his signal, and changed lanes again, almost striking a pickup truck. I told the trainee, "We're going to have to stop this guy now."

We turned on the blue lights to make a probable cause stop, and the vehicle sped up again. I thought he was going to run, but he suddenly pulled over and stopped. I could smell the alcohol by the time I reached the vehicle's trunk. The guy was so drunk it was remarkable he was still conscious. He was more than three times over the legal limit. Hoping to avoid being arrested, he told us he was a police officer—as if that was supposed to make a difference to me.

Another night we came across a vehicle that looked like it was broken down. We thought it had been abandoned until we got to the front and saw the driver standing there. The driver started telling us what was wrong with the vehicle, and while he was talking he urinated in the road. He was intoxicated—big surprise. Off to the jail we go.

74

Do You Mind If I Smoke?

One night while I still had this rookie with me another unit got dispatched to a natural-death call. My guy had worked only one such call since becoming a deputy, so I asked him if he wanted to do this for practice. He said, "Why not?" We called dispatch and said we would be taking the call for training purposes. We arrived at the address before the other unit. The trainee had started the report, so the other unit arrived as an assist.

The wife had gone to work and her husband was at the house. She worked the closing shift and came home late at night to find him dead. The assisting deputy probably had twenty-five years' experience at this time. He went into the house to look at the body to see if there was anything he could add to the report. Then he joined us on the front porch where we were trying to calm down the widow. The deceased looked a bit older than his wife but not that much older. The first thing the assisting deputy said to the woman was "Ma'am, is that your father?" She had just stopped blubbering long enough to tell us her name and his name and to give us basic information. Then he asked her that question, and she started wailing again. "That's my husband," she sobbed.

The assisting deputy made the best recovery I've ever seen anybody make in a situation like that. "Ma'am, do you mind if I smoke?" he asked. That was all it took. She pulled out one of her smokes to join him, and he gave her a light. I decided right then and there that would be my recovery line for any situation in which I put my foot in my mouth.

75

April 1998

In April 1998, an F-5 tornado came through the western part of Jefferson County. It did a tremendous amount of damage and killed a bunch of people. We were placed on twelve-hour shifts, and I was put in a roving car to relieve deputies who were manning parts of the area that were damaged and had been closed down. At the time the tornado hit, I was working the evening shift, and having been raised by a mother who sought shelter whenever she saw a gray cloud in the sky, I was quite attuned to the weather. I went to our substation because I could guess from reports that a tornado was heading toward our area.

The substation, a brick building, was low to the ground because there was a large hill right behind it. I figured that if the tornado made it that far, it would fly right off the hill and, worst case, pull off a few shingles. I sat at a desk with two large file cabinets on either side of it. I could take cover in this spot if the building collapsed. While I was sitting there the phone rang. Our patrol captain was on the other end. "It's getting kind of bad. Is everyone at the substation?" he asked.

"No sir," I said. "I'm the only person in here who's got any sense."

For almost a week after the tornado hit, parts of the area were closed off to everyone, even homeowners. The nights were long and sometimes boring. I pulled up to a lot where a house had been totally destroyed to have a sandwich and a drink. I turned off the headlights and turned on the inside dome light. After I had been sitting there for a while I thought I saw movement in the dark fifty to seventy-five feet away. I turned on the spotlight and saw the biggest rat I had ever seen. It was eight to eleven inches long without the tail. And it wasn't the only one. There were a bunch of them out there. I rolled down my window and pitched the rest of my sandwich their way. They were startled but didn't run. They started eating the sandwich like they were my pets.

I called the other deputy back to her area to show her the rats, and she admitted she hadn't seen them. She called another deputy working in the area, who happened to be on the SWAT team. He came down, and when he saw the rats he was just as shocked by their size and number. He had in his possession a silenced .22-caliber weapon used by the SWAT team to dispatch aggressive animals during raids. I left the area to go give another deputy a break, and the two deputies started thinning out the rat population. After the homeowners were allowed to return, we learned that one of them was raising rats as pets. Why? What's wrong with rabbits? They're cuter by most people's standards. I never found out if they killed the rat from that movie *Ben*.

76

Roach Killers

You visit some addresses on a regular basis if you work one area for very long. While I was on the night shift we went to one address on domestic calls at least every other week. When we got there we would find daddy had slapped around mama and had run off before we arrived. After making several visits, doing reports, and having mama refuse to sign warrants on him, we were getting tired of wasting our time. I had managed to get a DUI on this guy, but going to the house over and over with no results was becoming a pain.

One night a domestic call went out at the address and I was in the area. *We've got him this time*, I thought. I turned onto the road where the house was located, and as I neared the driveway I saw a male squatted down beside a tree across from the house. It was our suspect. He had already left and was watching for our arrival. He was holding a large hunting knife, and as I stopped in the road he ran off into the woods. My backup arrived a couple of minutes later. I have never been known for speed, and he knew the trails around the house, so he pretty much left me. As I was coming back out of the woods, I passed the tree where our suspect had been earlier. His hunting knife was stuck in the ground, and beside the tree was a fancy pair of pointy-toed cowboy boots. They looked fairly new. I guess he had run off barefoot.

My backup and I looked around in the woods but didn't find the guy that night. I got a call about a sexual assault on a minor about twenty miles away, so I had to leave. I remembered a story one of our veteran deputies had told me about a pair of cowboy boots and a rabbit they had a problem with, so I picked up the boots as I passed the tree and pitched them into the back of the patrol unit. I figured I could look for the owner when I finished the paperwork from these two calls.

I had to respond to an emergency room for the sexual assault call, and when I arrived there was a security guard standing by the entrance. There was also a garbage dumpster just a few feet away. I parked the patrol unit, got out my notebook to do my report, and grabbed the boots from the back as I walked toward the entrance. As I passed the dumpster, I tossed the boots in with all the coffee grinds and orange peels. Without breaking stride, I walked past the security guard and said, "How ya doing?" I went inside to take my report. I wonder if the security guard fished out the boots after I left.

77

Moove, Cow

Long before we had cars assigned to take home, we had cars assigned to the different beats, and the guys on each beat had to share a car. If we worked an outlying beat, we never got a new car because when a new car arrived at the substation it was assigned to one of the closer-to-town beats to show it off. My beat got the hand-me-down car.

One year the sheriff bought several new cars, and the outlying beat I worked finally got one. This was the first time I had driven a new unit. I thought all the cars came with spongy brakes, loose steering, worn-out shocks, and squeaky parts. The car had been assigned for less than a week when my off days came around. A chum who was my replacement on the beat called me after my first day off. He started the conversation by asking, "Are you real attached to that car?"

"Did you get hurt?" I asked.

"No, but the cow I hit didn't make it."

"Was the car totaled?" I asked.

"Nah. It was a glancing blow. He was in the middle of the travel lane, nothing was coming the other way, and I could swerve to avoid a direct hit."

Other than having to clean out his drawers, my chum was unharmed. We could also take heart because we wouldn't have to drive a wrecked car for long. The beat was so big we usually put more than a hundred thousand miles a year on a car, and it usually got replaced every year or so.

78

Rob, Are You in Here?

This story has nothing to do with law enforcement, but my wife thought it was so funny I decided to tell it. My wife was having trouble with her foot and eventually had to have surgery on it. During one of our doctor visits, I had to make an urgent trip to the restroom. I left the doctor's office and ducked quickly into the men's restroom in the hall. I went to the first of the two stalls and saw the lock was broken. I quickly stepped into the second stall and locked the door, just making it before the big moment. I sat there for a few minutes, making sure there weren't any aftershocks, when the restroom door opened and someone entered. I thought nothing of this except that this person would have to use the stall that wouldn't lock. After a short silence, I heard my wife say, "Rob, are you in here?"

"What are you doing in here?" I asked.

"This is the ladies room," she said.

"No, it's not," I told her.

"Yes, it is," she said and started to giggle.

"There's a men's sign on the door. I saw it," I said.

"No, there is not," she said, laughing.

She finished her business, washed her hands, and returned to the waiting room. I finished up and left the stall. I noticed then that there was no urinal in the room. Clue. I went out in the hall and looked at the door. Sure enough the sign said "Ladies." I entered the next room, labeled "Men," and washed my hands. I returned to the waiting room and sat next to my wife, who started giggling again. I told her that when I rushed into the restroom there was a "Men" sign on the door. I still say somebody swapped those signs. She still giggled about this when I took her for follow-up visits. "The men's restroom is on the left, not the right," she said.

79

What a Coincidence

A coincidence occurs when two things happening at random at the same time turn out to be related. While I was working as a detective we sometimes had to contact witnesses and suspects and to do lineups. On one case I had a possible witness who could put a burglary suspect in the area of the crime. I put a lineup together and was about to head out. A deputy I had worked with on the night shift was working light duty because of an injury, so I asked him if he wanted to ride with me. We got in the car and took a twenty-five- to thirty-minute ride to contact the witness. I knocked on the door, and a somewhat heavy-set young lady answered. She had one standout feature: her rear end was one of the widest I'd seen.

I talked with her about the case and found out that on the day of the burglary a male had knocked on her door. She said that when she went to the door, he asked her if she had seen a little brown dog in the area. He told her his dog had run away. She told him no and he left. This is a common practice of burglars. Knock on the door. If no one answers, kick it in. If someone answers, give the person a story like this one. I took a written statement from her and showed her a photo lineup. I thanked her, and we got back in the unit to leave as she walked up the steps to her residence.

We had parked just at her front door, so when we started the car to leave she was in front of the windshield. We heard the first few bars of the Queen song "Fat Bottomed Girls" on the radio as I was putting the car in reverse. There we were with this view in front of us with that song playing. It couldn't have been a more fitting song. What a coincidence. We laughed like we had never seen anything funny before.

80

Repeat Customers

I can't get over the fact that when arrests are made for domestic abuse, in about 90 percent of the cases the victims want the judge to drop the charges. One night we answered a call to one of our regular domestic violence addresses. We had been to this house several times, and each time the husband had knocked around or pushed the wife. This time as we rolled up he was over her on the floor, beating her with a short-barreled shotgun. We started toward him, and he ran off toward the back of the residence where their child was sleeping.

Thinking he had taken the child as a hostage or as a human shield, we posted up at different corners until other units arrived. We found out he didn't have the child hostage, and we searched a wooded area until we found him. This turned out to be about a seven-hour ordeal. He had dropped the shotgun, but we recovered it. We took him to jail on a first-degree assault charge and for various misdemeanors. He had beaten his wife with the shotgun until he broke the stock on her.

It was about midway through the shift when we got the call and after daylight when we found him and took him to jail. Between taking him to jail, going to the district attorney's office, and doing the paperwork, I wound up working about six hours overtime. When I got home I went to bed and slept until it was time to return to work. When I got to roll call, there was a call from the victim. She was asking me to drop the charges and to let her husband out of jail. I told her that wasn't something I would do if it were up to me but that only the judge could do something like that.

She wasn't happy with my answer and asked to speak with my supervisor. I put her on hold and told the sergeant she didn't like my answer and wanted to talk to him. He got on the phone to see if he could explain the situation to her, and when she wasn't happy with the same answer she got from me, she started cussing him like a dog. She called him everything but a child of God. She ended up calling the district attorney's office before it was over but still with no luck. True love.

81

Stop, or I'll Scream like a Girl

One night I was working with one of my chums in a two-man unit, and we were checking businesses. We went by a burger store and saw a man chasing a woman inside. The place was closed, so no one should have been inside but the employees who were cleaning up. We circled around, thinking this might be a domestic incident. Maybe an employee had let a spouse inside to wait until after work. As we pulled up to the other side, we saw the man had a gun and was chasing after the employees. We had rolled up to a robbery in progress.

We leaped out with our weapons in hand. All the doors were locked, but there was one on the opposite side of the building that would open from the inside to let you out but would lock behind you when you exited. Thinking the man was going that way, we ran around the building. He already had about a thirty-yard lead on us. He slowed down at a car parked near the burger joint (which turned out to be his getaway car) but then ran past the vehicle. If he had stopped we would have had him. Because we were not built for speed and this guy was built like a gazelle, he completely out ran us. We trailed behind, yelling for him to stop or we would shoot.

The guy got away that night but was later caught. But we got his car, and we had plenty of other evidence. He had jumped the stainless steel counter that one of the employees had just cleaned, and he left a full handprint for our evidence technician to collect. Later I told my chum that I would never again chase after anyone with the command "Stop, or I'll shoot." Next time my command of choice would be "Stop, or I'll scream like a girl."

82

The Family That Weeds Together

Once while I was working the evening shift we received a call from dispatch about a man with a warrant at a certain location. Our office is always getting these calls, and usually they're from women who have gotten mad at an ex-hubby or a boyfriend and have called to rat the guy out. Hell hath no fury like a woman scorned. After roll call three of us went over to the address given and knocked on the door. A male in his midtwenties answered, and we asked for the person whose name we had. There was also an older male just inside. The man who answered the door said that this was his name and his dad's and that they were both there.

After a call to dispatch to check on a birth date on the warrant, we learned we were looking for the younger man. But his father also caught our interest because when his son opened the door,

Dad was sitting on the couch just inside the living room at the coffee table peeling marijuana off the stems and placing it in small bags. He didn't bother to cover up just because the sheriff was at the door. Also, the younger child of the man we were looking for was standing at the coffee table, watching all this go on. He was a toddler around two and a half.

We ended up taking both the son and the dad to jail. We had to call someone to come get the child. They had about twenty bags packed up and stored in a cigar box in addition to what they were working on. They also had scales. We brought in a drug dog to find out if there was more. The dog handler had to take the dog out because even though we had found all that was there at the time, there had been so much marijuana inside the house that the dog was going crazy sniffing around. I've always said that after working this job for a while nothing shocks me anymore, but some things still surprise me.

83

No More Blue-Light Warnings

At one point in my law enforcement career, I got pretty good at letting cars get stolen from out in front of me. But this was usually when I had a trainee with me. One night I was riding around with a trainee, and we'd had a pretty good month. We'd made several arrests for DUI, public drunkenness, and domestic violence and had written several tickets for speeding tickets and for revoked licenses. We were going to a call and were running the moving radar while en route.

We clocked one vehicle speeding and hit the blue lights to slow it down. The trainee was driving, and nothing was behind us, so he slowed the car to turn around. I told him to continue to the call. He wasn't lacking for cases, so if he wanted to let this one slide he wouldn't be hurting. The trainee said, "I don't think he slowed down. I think he even sped up." As the vehicle passed us, we noticed it was a black Ford Mustang with a convertible top. We also decided against going after the driver because another vehicle was a few seconds behind him. We would not have been directly behind the vehicle if we turned around.

We went on to the call, and as we finished up with it, an off-duty deputy from our sheriff's office called the dispatcher to report someone had crashed a car into a fence on his property. The deputy gave the dispatcher the tag, and the car it was assigned to turned out to be a Saturn. The deputy said no one was around the vehicle. After the crash, the driver ran off. The deputy lived on the beat we were working, so I told the trainee to start that way. We joked that it would be funny if the car was the Mustang we had clocked on radar. I told him the tag had come from a Saturn.

We arrived at the scene and found a black Ford Mustang with a convertible top. The driver had laid down about seventy-five feet of rubber straightening out a curve. He jumped a four-foot ditch as he caught a road sign. He had to be airborne, and when he landed, he was about fifteen feet from the shoulder of the road. He dumped the road sign at this point but only after it peeled the fender like a can opener. Two pieces of the Mustang lay on the ground along with the driver's window, which had been knocked out by the sign. The driver traveled about another hundred feet before he was able to stop the vehicle. The airbag had deployed. He had taken a pretty good ride. The steering column was busted.

I told the trainee as we pulled up, "I've been seeing that car somewhere, but I can't think where." As we started the report, we saw For Sale signs on the floor of the car. We collected those and other items for our evidence guys to process. I called the number on the For Sale sign, and after several rings, a male voice came on the phone. I asked whom I was speaking with, and the name matched the registered owner's. I asked if he owned a black Mustang, and he replied he did and told me where he had it parked for sale. I told him I hated to be the bearer of bad news but that it was about two miles from that spot and it had been wrecked. "It's been stolen," he said. (I always want to say, "No. We think it may have run away on its own.")

I told him where the vehicle was being taken and said he should contact his insurance company and let it handle the details. We wrote our report and took our evidence to turn it in. I told the trainee, "Next time if we light one up, we're going to stop it. No more blue-light warnings." But I remembered where I had seen that Mustang.

www.ingramcontent.com/pod-product-compliance
Lightning Source LLC
Chambersburg PA
CBHW030919180526
45163CB00002B/391